René Descartes

Ethics

René Descartes

Ethics

Edited and Translated by
Roger Ariew

Hackett Publishing Company, Inc.
Indianapolis/Cambridge

Copyright © 2024 by Hackett Publishing Company, Inc.

All rights reserved
Printed in the United States of America

27 26 25 24   1 2 3 4 5 6 7

For further information, please address
Hackett Publishing Company, Inc.
P.O. Box 44937
Indianapolis, Indiana 46244-0937

www.hackettpublishing.com

Cover design by Listenberger Design & Associates
Interior design by Laura Clark
Composition by Aptara, Inc.

Library of Congress Control Number: 2023941586

ISBN-13: 978-1-64792-157-6 (pbk.)
ISBN-13: 978-1-64792-158-3 (PDF ebook)
ISBN-13: 978-1-64792-159-0 (epub)

The paper used in this publication meets the minimum requirements of American National Standard for Information Sciences—Permanence of Paper for Printed Library Materials, ANSI Z39.48–1984.

∞

Contents

General Introduction — ix

Notes on the Edition and Translation — xxiii

Abbreviations — xxvi

Chapter I — 1

  The Greatest Good, Descartes to Christina (November 20, 1647) — 1

  The Happy Life, Descartes to Elisabeth (August 4, 1645) — 3

  How the Understanding Is Confirmed in Its Knowledge That the Greatest Good Lies in the Actions of Life, Descartes to Elisabeth (September 15, 1645) — 7

  Whether in This Life There Are More Goods than Evils, Descartes to Elisabeth [January 1646] — 10

  Free Will, Descartes to Mersenne (May 27, 1641) — 11

Chapter II — 14

  The Passions in General, *Passions of the Soul* (1649), Part I — 14

  The Specific Passions, *Passions of the Soul*, Part II — 25
    Wonder — 27
    Love and Hatred — 29
    Desire — 31
    Joy — 32
    Sadness — 33

  The Passions Following from the Primitive Passions, *Passions of the Soul*, Part III — 36
    The Passions Following from Wonder — 36
    The Passions Following from Love and Hatred — 41
    The Passions Following from Desire, Joy, and Sadness — 43

Chapter III — 50

What Is Love? Descartes to Chanut (February 1, 1647) — 50

Whether Natural Light Alone Teaches Us to Love God?
Descartes to Chanut (Ibid.) — 53

What Are the Causes Often Inciting Us to Love Someone in Preference to Another before We Know His Merit? Descartes to Chanut (June 6, 1647) — 55

Which of Two Disorders Is Worse, That of Love or That of Hatred? Descartes to Chanut (February 1, 1647) — 56

The Joy of the Soul, Descartes to Elisabeth [November 1646] — 58

Whether It Is Better to Be Joyful and Content, Imagining the Goods We Possess to Be Greater and More Valuable Than They Are, Than to Have More Consideration and Knowledge, and Know the Right Value of Both and Thus to Grow Sadder? Descartes to Elisabeth (October 6, 1645) — 59

Appendix — 61

The Provisional Morals, *Discourse on Method*, Part III (1637) — 61

Two Questions about the Provisional Morals — 66
    From S. P. to [Reneri] for Descartes [April 1638] — 66
    From Descartes to [Reneri] for S. P. [May 1638] — 66

The Longevity of Life and Morals, Descartes to Mersenne (January 9, 1639) — 69

From the Letters by Elisabeth to Descartes — 69
    Elisabeth to Descartes (August 16 [1645]) — 69
    Elisabeth to Descartes (September 13 [1645]) — 70
    Elisabeth to Descartes (September 30 [1645]) — 71
    Elisabeth to Descartes (October 28 [1645]) — 72
    Elisabeth to Descartes [November 30, 1645] — 75
    Elisabeth to Descartes (April 25 [1646]) — 76

From the Letters between Descartes and Chanut — 77
    Descartes to Chanut (June 15, 1646) — 77
    Chanut to Descartes (August 25, 1646) — 78

Chanut to Descartes (December 1, 1646)   79
Chanut to Descartes (May 11, 1647)   80
Descartes to Chanut (November 20, 1647)   82

The Tree of Philosophy, from the Preface to *Principles of Philosophy* (1647)   83

From a Prefatory Letter to the *Passions of the Soul* (1649)   86

Concerning the *Treatise on the Passions,* Descartes to Clerselier [April 23, 1649]   87

General Introduction

1. Text and Context

This volume is an edition and translation of Renati Des-Cartes, *Ethice. In Methodum et Compendium, Gratiâ Studiosae juventutis, Concinnata* (London, 1685)—henceforth referred to as Descartes's *Ethics*. Descartes never wrote such a book, but its anonymous editor was able to put together a three-part treatise out of Descartes's own words (translated from French into Latin) using his correspondence with Queen Christina of Sweden, Princess Elisabeth of Bohemia, and Pierre Chanut,[1] and the published Latin translation of *Passions of the Soul*.[2] The beginning of Descartes's *Ethics* concerns the supreme good, the happy life, and free will.[3] And the end contains a discourse on intellectual and sensitive love and the love of

---

1. It may look as though the anonymous editor made a concerted selection from Descartes's letters, but in fact he was just following Claude Clerselier's edition, *Lettres de Mr Descartes*, 3 vols. (Paris, 1657–1667)—henceforth abbreviated as "Clerselier"—or, more precisely, its Latin translation published in Amsterdam and London in 1668—henceforth abbreviated as *"Epistolae."* (*Epistolae* usually follows Clerselier's numbering of the letters.) The main edition of Descartes's works is *Oeuvres de Descartes* by Charles Adam and Paul Tannery, 11 vols. (Paris: Vrin, 1969). Henceforth abbreviated "AT, volume, page." Page number references to the AT edition are given in the margins.
2. *Passiones Animae*, Posthumous ed. (Amsterdam, 1650) by an anonymous translator; the title page says "ab H.D.M.I.V.L.", probably standing for "*by Henricus Des-Marets, Iuris Vtrusque Licentiatus*"—see the Introduction by J.-R. Armogathe and G. Belgioioso to *Passiones animae* (Facsimile ed., Lecce: Conte Editore, 1997). The original French-language treatise was published in Paris and Amsterdam in November 1649, about three months before Descartes's death on February 11, 1650.
3. 1. *De summo bono* (from a letter to Christina, November 20, 1647, AT V, 82–85, Clerselier 1). 2. *De vita beata* (from the following letters to Elisabeth: August 4, 1645, AT IV, 264–66, Clerselier 4; September 1, 1645, AT IV, 281–87, Clerselier 6; September 15, 1645, AT IV, 291–96, Clerselier 7; January 1646, AT IV, 354–56, Clerselier 10). 3. *De libero arbitrio* (from the following letters to Mersenne or Mesland: May 27, 1641, AT III, 378–80, Clerselier 112 (Latin version Descartes to [Mesland?] [February 9, 1645?], AT IV, 173–75); May 2, 1644, AT IV, 117, Clerselier 115; and to Elisabeth: January 1646, AT IV, 354, Clerselier 10; November 3, 1645, AT IV, 332, Clerselier 7).

ix

God.[4] In between these essays constructed from the correspondence is an abbreviated, and at times reordered version from all three parts of *Passions of the Soul*, with the physiological passages deleted. For example, completely missing are the articles on the parts of the body and their functions, the motion of the heart, the animal spirits in the brain, the motion of the muscles, and the sense organs.[5] Also missing are the articles about the order and enumeration of the passions and about the physiological effects of the passions on the body.[6] The largest section of this middle portion of Descartes's *Ethics* concerns Part 3 of *Passions of the Soul*, which is the smallest portion of Descartes's treatise,[7] but the one most devoted to moral philosophy.

Descartes's *Ethics* seems to have found readers in London and Cambridge, having been republished, together with *Synopsis Ethices* by Etienne de Courcelles (1586–1659), in a single volume (London, 1702), and then both together with *Ethica, sive Moralis Disciplinae* by Eustachius a Sancto Paulo (1573–1640), that is, Part 2 of Eustachius's *Summa Philosophiae Quadripartita* (1609, and numerous editions until 1649). In this latter tripartite compendium (Cambridge, 1707), the first part given is the *Ethica* of the Catholic Scholastic Eustachius whose *Summa* Descartes called "the best book of its kind,"[8] the second, the *Synopsis Ethices* of the Protestant

---

4. Starting with a fragment of a letter to Chanut (February 1, 1647, AT IV, 601–6, Clerselier 35), *Quid sit amor?* and continuing with a discussion of topics such as: *Utrum solo lumine naturali Deum amare doceamur* (To Chanut, February 1, 1647, 1 Feb. 1647, AT IV, 607–13, Clerselier 35); *Quae sint causae quibus ad hominem unum magis quam alium, etiam incognitis meritis, amandum ferimur* (To Chanut, June 6, 1647, AT V, 56–58, Clerselier 36); *Uter sit deterior, amoris an odii excessus?* (To Chanut, February 1, 1647, AT IV, 613–17, Clerselier 35); *De laeto animo* (To Elisabeth, October or November 1646, AT IV, 529–30, Clerselier 15); *An satius est laeto esse animo et contento imaginando ea, quae possidemus bona majora et meliora, quam sunt; an vero accuratius pensitare justum utrorumque valorem, atque inde tristitiam contrahere?* (To Elisabeth, October 6, 1645, AT IV, 305–9: Clerselier 8).

5. Missing as well are articles 34–38 about the pineal gland.

6. Except for the first sentence from Art. 107 and the title and last sentence of Art. 112.

7. Part 3 of *Passions of the Soul* is just under twenty-seven pages, while Parts 1 and 2 are twenty-seven and forty-two pages, respectively. In the London textbook, chap. 1, De passionibus in genere, is nineteen pages, chap. 2, De passionibus in specie, eighteen pages, and chap. 3, De illis passionibus, quae primitivas sequuntur, twenty-eight pages.

8. See Roger Ariew, "*Le meilleur livre qui ait jamais été fait en cette matière*: Eustachius a Sancto Paulo and the Teaching of Philosophy in the Seventeenth Century," *Teaching Philosophy in Early Modern Europe: Text and Image*, in *Archimedes*, ed. Susanna Berger and Daniel Garber (Springer, 2022), 31–46.

theologian de Courcelles, a friend of Descartes and translator of the *Discourse on Method* (*Specimina Philosophiae*) into Latin, and the third, the *Ethice* of Descartes, which, as we will see, focuses on humans and what they can do to live happily in this life.[9]

There are several reasons why Descartes's *Ethics* is significant (as are all three parts of the 1707 compendium). Descartes did not say much about ethics or happiness in his published works; there is, of course, his "provisional" morals in *Discourse*, Part 3, and his thoughts about how we can best comport ourselves in *Passions of the Soul*, Part 3. According to the *Conversation with Burman*, on April 16, 1648, Descartes was asked about his provisional code of ethics in the *Discourse*. He supposedly replied, "The author does not willingly write about ethics, but was forced to include these rules for the sake of pedagogues and others, who would have said that he is someone without religion or faith, and that he intended to subvert people through his method."[10] This statement has been taken to show Descartes's great uneasiness about writing on ethics and morals, one perhaps as great as his reluctance to write about religion and revealed theology, that is, truths dependent on supernatural, not natural light. Although the *Conversation with Burman* statement seems to be limited to the provisional morals of 1637, Descartes did say something similar and more general in a letter to Chanut from November 20, 1647: "It is true that I usually refuse to write down my thoughts concerning morality. There are two reasons for this. One is that there is no other matter on which malicious people can more easily derive pretexts for slandering; the other is that I believe it belongs only to sovereigns, or those authorized by them, to concern themselves in regulating the customs

---

9. The actual texts given in the 1707 Cambridge compendium were Eustachius's *Ethica*, together with the two texts of the 1702 Cambridge work, that is, the third edition of de Courcelles's *Synopsis ethices* with the second edition of Descartes's *Ethice*. The first edition of de Courcelles was likely the one published in his *Opera Theologica* (Amsterdam, 1675), 982–1018, with the second edition being the stand-alone volume published in London in 1684—all posthumous publications. The first edition of Descartes was the volume from 1685. As for Eustachius's *Ethica*, as we said, it was the second part of his *Summa Philosophiae Quadripartita*, which was published first in 1609 and republished numerous times until 1649 whether as a single volume, or two volumes of two parts each, or four separate parts (including editions in Cambridge, from 1640 to 1649); the *Ethica* was republished by itself many times in London between 1654 and 1693 before being incorporated into the 1707 Cambridge compendium.

10. AT V, 178.

of others."[11] This more general assertion was however being uttered at a time when Descartes was revealing his thoughts on ethics, and in particular his views about the supreme good or happiness. Replying to himself, Descartes continued, "But these two reasons do not apply to the opportunity you did me the honor of giving me, by writing on behalf of the incomparable Queen [Christina] whom you serve, that it pleases her if I write to her about my opinion regarding the supreme good."[12] In fact, Descartes was sending to Christina all the letters he had already written to Princess Elisabeth on the subject, to accompany the one he wrote specifically for her (that is, Descartes to Elisabeth, July 21, 1645, August 4, 1645, August 18, 1645, September 1, 1645, September 15, 1645, and October 6, 1645, to accompany Descartes to Christina, November 20, 1647).[13] Descartes even attached a manuscript version of his *Passions of the Soul*, which he claimed to provide foundations for his ethics: "And I include a little *Treatise on the Passions*, which is not the least part of the collection; for it is primarily the passions we must try to understand in order to obtain the supreme good I described."[14] Thus, Descartes did not say much about ethics in his *published* works, but that does not mean he was uninterested in the subject and did not write about it extensively in his *unpublished* correspondence. The set of letters Descartes sent to Christina, together with the *Passions of the Soul* and the subsequent letters Descartes wrote to Chanut for Christina, constitute the bulk of Descartes's *Ethics*.

Descartes did intend ultimately to complete a treatise on morals. As he said in the preface to the French edition of the *Principles*,

> I believe myself to have begun to explain the whole of philosophy in proper order [. . .]. To carry this plan to a conclusion, I should afterward in the same way explain in further detail the nature of each of the other bodies on the earth, that is, minerals, plants, animals, and above all man, then finally treat exactly of medicine, morals, and mechanics. All

---

11. AT V, 86–87.
12. AT V, 87.
13. Respectively, AT IV, 251–53, 263–68, 271–78, 281–87, 290–96, and 304–17, and AT V, 81–86.
14. AT V, 87.

this I should have to do in order to give to mankind a complete body of philosophy.[15]

This is an extension of Descartes's metaphor of a tree of philosophy from the same preface, in which one is gathering fruits from the tree, which requires the establishment of the tree's metaphysical roots, its physical trunk, and its branches constituted by medicine, mechanics, and morals. The problem however is that, as Descartes said, he did not perform sufficient experiments to finish the trunk. Thus, he could not endeavor to venture onto its nonexistent branches; that is, he could not write treatises on medicine and morality until he had solved a variety of problems concerning animals and humans. As a result, he needed to limit himself to some fairly disconnected thoughts about the good, happiness, and virtue in his correspondence, and he died before he could sort out his thoughts fully.

The anonymous editor of Descartes's *Ethice* performs an important task by piecing out Descartes's thoughts about ethics, "compiling, ordering, and abridging them," as he indicates. This is not a trivial matter since it requires knowledge of Descartes's correspondence. Clearly, an adequate understanding of what might constitute a Cartesian ethics needed to await Claude Clerselier's posthumous publication of Descartes's letters (the three volumes of *Lettres de Mr Descartes,* 1657–1667). Moreover, Clerselier's collection of letters was not simply a random selection (or a chronologically ordered set of letters, as we would publish), but the result of Clerselier's wanting to construct new Cartesian texts to fill the gaps in the extant corpus, starting with ethics. Clerselier's first volume of Descartes's correspondence begins with a 1647 letter to Christina on the supreme good and continues with the letters to Elisabeth from 1645 on

---

15. AT IXb, 17. The desire to work on morals seems to be a late development in Descartes's thought. While initially mechanics and medicine were primary as means for living a longer and happier life—see Descartes to Huygens (December 4, 1637), AT I, 649; Descartes to Mersenne (January 9, 1639), AT II, 480; and the end of *Discourse* VI—it took a while for morals to be included. In the end, however, Descartes turned fully to the subject; as he said to Pierre Chanut in 1646: "I will tell you, in confidence, that the notion of physics I tried to develop served me tremendously in establishing foundations in morals that are certain; I more easily satisfied myself on this point than on many others concerning medicine, on which I nevertheless spent much more time. As such, instead of finding the means for preserving life, I found something else, easier and surer, which is to not fear death." Descartes to Chanut (June 15, 1646), AT IV, 441.

the happy life. In his preface to the volume Clerselier even argues that his collection of Descartes's letters is equivalent to any other of Descartes's writings, since "one should not fear the public censure of what is written for Princesses and for the most learned people in Europe. What is addressed to such people, who are esteemed for their rank, knowledge, or virtue, will assuredly be well-considered and highly polished." Clerselier then asserts that the highest and most useful subject is the one Descartes examines in his letter to Queen Christina, namely, the topic of the supreme good, which he treated as well in the letters to Princess Elisabeth. Clerselier writes:

> Descartes allowed people to see, in these letters, that ethics was one of his most common meditations, and that he was not so powerfully engaged with the consideration of things that happen up in the air, or with the inquiry into the secret paths nature observes in the production of its works here below, such that he failed to reflect frequently on himself, and [. . .] to regulate the actions of his life, following the true reason. [. . .] After this, I do not think that anyone will be able to accuse him of vanity in his studies, as being completely engaged with an inquiry into the empty things of which science fills the mind, instead of those that instruct and perfect man.[16]

Before Clerselier's collection of Descartes's correspondence, there is little that could be said about Descartes's ethics. This thought can be illustrated by the first "Cartesian" ethics written just after the death of Descartes and before the publication of his correspondence.

Jacques Du Roure has the distinction of having written the first Cartesian textbook, which includes an *Ethics* or *Moral Philosophy* (published in 1654, before Clerselier, vol. 1). The *Morale* from his *Philosophy* discusses the opinion of scholars both inside and outside the Schools.[17] And, in its portion on felicity, Du Roure devotes a chapter to the supreme good, explaining Scholastic doctrine, but also adding sections on the views of Gassendi and Descartes.[18] The Descartes fragment happens to be

---

16. Clerselier, vol. 1, unpaginated preface.
17. Jacques Du Roure, *La Philosophie divisée en toutes ses parties, établie sur des principes évidents et expliquée en tables et discours, ou particuliers, ou tirés des anciens et des nouveaux auteurs, et principalement des péripatéticiens et de Descartes* (Paris, 1654), II, 283–84.
18. For Gassendi, see Du Roure, La Philosophie, II, 314–17; for Descartes, 317–20.

a summary of Descartes's letter to Elisabeth of August 4, 1645;[19] as Du Roure states, "Descartes teaches, in his letters to Princess Elisabeth, that natural beatitude consists in having the mind perfectly content."[20] Du Roure then, following Descartes, distinguishes between good fortune and happiness, and lists three maxims useful for acquiring felicity. It is interesting that Du Roure knows this letter before its publication in Clerselier; but he does not seem to be aware of Descartes's other letters about these matters. In the article on freedom from the section on virtues and vices, Du Roure details Descartes's view about freedom of indifference, as given in a letter of May 27, 1641.[21] And in the section on passions, he devotes a whole chapter to the passions, according to Descartes, their definition and number, causes and effects, and remedies.[22] Du Roure concludes his *Morale* with a lengthy section called Moral Philosophy Demonstrated, which is advertised by Du Roure as being inspired by Descartes and Hobbes,[23] but really comes directly from Hobbes (from the *De cive*). Despite Du Roure's enthusiasm, it is unlikely that Descartes and Hobbes could be made to fit under the same umbrella.[24] Even though he knows two important unpublished letters of Descartes and the published *Passions of the Soul*, Du Roure is not able to construct a Cartesian ethics; his *Morale* gives the impression of something that did not fully come together.

2. Ethics in Descartes and the Cartesians

Following Clerselier's volumes of *Letters* there appeared an important anonymous work indebted to Clerselier. The work, titled *L'art de vivre heureux formé sur les idées les plus claires de la raison et du sens commun et sur de très belles maximes de Monsieur Descartes*, constructs a Cartesian-style ethics from a variety of sources, but especially from Descartes's letters to Christina and to Elisabeth, prominently displayed in Clerselier's correspondence. The treatise discusses man's happiness in this life here below.

---

19. That is, Clerselier's letter 4, AT IV. 264–66; cf. Descartes, *Ethice*, chap. 1, sec. 2.
20. Du Roure, *La Philosophie*, II, 317.
21. Also prior to its publication in Clerselier, as Clerselier 112 (AT III, 378–82). This is the French version of the Latin letter to Mesland of February 9, 1645, AT IV, 173–75. Du Roure's exposition is in 1654, ii, 340–44. Cf. Descartes, *Ethice*, chap. 1, sec. 4.
22. Du Roure, *La Philosophie*, II, 415–55.
23. Du Roure, *La Philosophie*, II, 458.
24. See Descartes to an Unknown Jesuit [May 1642–July 1644], AT IV, 68.

The author sets aside the supernatural happiness of saints, in the state of grace, and makes room for a natural and rational kind of happiness that can be attained in this life, despite our fallen state. He argues that there are goods to be attained here below, apart from grace and faith, which, though useless for salvation, permit us to perform morally good acts. These preliminaries allow the author to continue with an extended paraphrase of Descartes's 1647 letter to Christina: the only supreme absolute good is God; but there are goods relative to us that depend on us (such as virtue and wisdom) and those independent of us (such as honors, riches, and health), that is, goods of the body and fortune. Happiness or the most solid contentment consists in what is in our power, that is, the goods of our mind: knowing and willing. The anonymous author continues his treatise with a discussion of the nature of the human soul. He calls Aristotle's opinion on the subject "dangerous and obscure"[25] and adopts the Augustinian-Cartesian view that "the soul is a substance that has only thought as attribute, from which one concludes that it is spiritual and immortal."[26] He follows with a few chapters on Cartesian animal-machines and concludes with materials on the two faculties of the soul, understanding and will, again following Descartes. The end of the treatise rejoins the discussion of ethics with an extended paraphrase of the letters to Elisabeth, and lists three conditions useful for acquiring felicity: trying always to use our minds as well as possible to discover what we should do in all the circumstances of our lives; having a firm and constant resolution to execute everything reason advises us, without allowing our passions or appetites to divert us; and considering that while we are conducting ourselves in this manner, the goods we do not possess are entirely outside our power.[27] In those letters, given our imperfect knowledge, the further truths we need to keep in mind in order to judge well are the existence of God, the nature of our souls, and our distinctness from every part of the universe. Here, these are understood as the three principal truths by which to guide our conduct toward God, the self, and others, namely: there is a God, on which all things depend; know thyself, that is, you should know the nature of your soul; and you should

---

25. *L'art de vivre heureux, formé sur les idées les plus claires de la raison et du sens commun et sur de très belles maximes de Monsieur Descartes*, ed. Sébastien Charles (Paris: Vrin, 2009 [1st ed. 1687]), 67; see also 67–73. The work is anonymous, though it is often attributed to the Oratorian Claude Ameline.
26. *L'art de vivre heureux*, 73; see also 73–76.
27. *L'art de vivre heureux*, 53–58 and 113–15.

prefer the interests of the whole to your specific interests. For the anonymous author, the passions enter the discussion only insofar as they can trouble the will, whose constancy constitutes virtue. Although providing a limited perspective and departing from Descartes's view that morals is a science, the author of *The Art of Living Happily* seems to have understood Descartes reasonably well, delineating an anthropocentric ethics based on the Cartesian view of the soul and its two functions, all in parallel with and apart from a theocentric, supernatural ethics and contrasting with Aristotle's naturalistic ethics.

Descartes's *Ethics* provides a broader perspective on Descartes's views of happiness than does *The Art of Living Happily*, since it adds materials about the passions (from *Passions of the Soul*) and on love (from the Letters to Chanut and Elisabeth) to Descartes's treatment of happiness (from the letters to Christina and Elisabeth). While it does not directly address the question of whether ethics is a science or an art, it also does not assert that it is an art, as does *The Art of Living Happily*, which, although it bills itself as "based on the beautiful maxims of Mr. Descartes," clearly departs from his view that it is a science, even the ultimate science based on all the other sciences.

This beginning of a Cartesian ethics allows a clear contrast between Descartes's morals and late Scholastic ethics. Descartes and the Scholastics apparently agree that ethics is a science, and not an art, and not the same as prudence—that is, advice about how best to behave in specific situations. The contrast between Cartesian and Scholastic views about happiness is somewhat harder to delineate, mainly because, as expected, Scholastics did not seem to agree on any single position about happiness. One can still find a few writers, such as Scipion Dupleix and Théophraste Bouju, defending the naturalistic Aristotelian intellectualist view of happiness as activity of the soul in conformity with excellence or virtue.[28] And one can find others, such as the Jesuits of Coimbra, defending the mixed naturalistic and theocentric Thomistic intellectualist view, dividing happiness into two: natural, or Aristotelian and imperfect; and supernatural, or perfect, with supernatural happiness residing in the understanding and consisting of contemplation of the divine essence.[29] There is also a variety of

---

28. Scipion Dupleix, *L'éthyque*, ed. R. Ariew (Paris, 1993; 1st ed., 1610), 131 and 135–38, and Théophraste Bouju, *Corps de toute la philosophie* (Paris, 1614), Morale, 34–39.
29. Conimbricenses, *In libros Ethicorum Aristotelis ad Nicomachum aliquot Cursus disputationes* (Lisbon, 1593), 26–28.

theocentric Scotist voluntarist views, in which happiness consists in the love of God, which is an act of the will.[30] But there is, as well, a new seventeenth-century Scholastic position that is somewhat different from all of these and could be described as a consensus doctrine. The general agreement, accepted by such diverse thinkers as Eustachius a Sancto Paulo, the ex-Jesuit René de Ceriziers, the Thomist Antoine Goudin, and the Scotist Claude Frassen, is resolutely theocentric: happiness is divided into objective happiness, which has God as its object, and formal happiness, whether natural or supernatural, which is a state residing in the intellect and requiring both of its faculties: the understanding and the will. There is still some division over whether the essence of that formal happiness resides principally in the understanding, that is, in the vision of the divine essence, which entails the love of God, or more principally in the love of God, that is, an act of the will, which also requires the contemplation of God, or both. These views provide a sharp contrast with Cartesian morals, even with the limited perspective of the *Art of Living Happily*.[31]

Antoine Le Grand (1629–1699) also used Clerselier's work to construct a Cartesian ethics as part of his textbooks intended to teach a

---

30. Claude Frassen, *Philosophia Academica, quam ex selectissimis Aristotelis et Doctoris Subtilis Scoti rationibus ac sententiis* (Paris, 1668; 1st ed., 1657), IV, 57–62.
31. De Courcelle's *Synopsis Ethices* offers a contrast with both Eustachius and Descartes on ethics. In his first chapter (I. *De Natura Ethices*), de Courcelles argues that ethics is the science of mores, allowing people to strive toward happiness, and differentiates it from wisdom and prudence. The genus of ethics is science (not art) and its difference from other sciences is that its subject is mores and human happiness. The parts of ethics are virtues and happiness. There are two species of ethics, one philosophical, the other theological; the former in conformity with natural light, and about happiness in this life, and the latter dealing with the Christian virtues of faith, hope, and charity, and about our happiness in heaven. But, de Courcelles argues, no one who neglects celestial happiness can be happy in this life. While de Courcelles produces a seemingly standard Scholastic account of ethics, the emphasis is clearly on the theological part, that is, on Christian revelation. This is made clear in his final chapter on happiness (XV. *De Beatitudine*), where de Courcelles issues the same kinds of provisos as the Scholastics about the supreme good and the conditions for it and argues that it does not consist in the goods of fortune, the body, pleasure, or even knowledge and virtue. He asserts (correctly as we indicated) that the Scholastics consider the supreme good in a dual fashion, that is, both objective, which is God himself, and formal, which is the enjoyment of God. But he states that the distinction is improper: to say that God is our objective supreme good is to make God an object; and if God is the object of the supreme good, he is not himself the supreme good and cannot be enjoyed in himself.

complete curriculum of Cartesian philosophy for his students in London.[32] In the preface to the last part of his *Institution of Philosophy*, on *Ethicks*, Le Grand states: "I would also have the Reader take notice, that in this Treatise I follow the Sentiments of DESCARTES: and tho' he hath writ but little concerning *Moral Philosophy*, yet I have a mind to raise this structure upon the Foundation he hath laid, and from what he hath Writ concerning the *Soul of Man*, and the *Passions* to discover his Sense of *Moral Matters*."[33] As Le Grand says, he believes he can represent a complete Cartesian physics, including parts on man, both in respect to his body and in respect to his mind or soul, as a ground for a Cartesian ethics. Thus, after treating man in relation to his body and soul and discussing passions of the soul, Le Grand produces a Cartesian ethics, with considerations of such topics as the greatest good, the nature of virtue, the usefulness of the passions, their governance, and the more general remedies for them. He begins by arguing that external goods are not the good of man, and comes to the main question: What is the highest good and ultimate end of man in this life? He distinguishes between mankind and private man and asserts that the supreme good for mankind is the concurrence of all perfections of which he is capable, the goods of the soul and body and fortune. But for private man the supreme good is the right use of his reason, which consists in "his having a firm and constant purpose of always doing that, which he judges to be the best." This, of course, is in our power, whereas the goods of body and fortune are not. The proper use of our two main intellectual faculties also produces a satisfaction of mind. The doctrine is encapsulated in the three things we need to observe, which are said to be the foundation of all ethics. The first is that we "strive to attain the *Knowledge* of what we ought to embrace." The second is that "we stand firm and constant to what we have once resolved upon and purposed; that is, that we retain an

---

32. Le Grand's textbooks include *Philosophia veterum e mente Renati Descartes, more scholastico breviter digesta* (London, 1671), its successor *Institutio philosophia, secundum principia Renati Descartes . . . ad usum juventutis academicae* (in numerous editions, London, 1672, 1675, 1678, 1680; Nuremberg, 1679, 1683, 1695, and 1711; Geneva, 1694), and ultimately the latter's English translation and revision as *Institution of Philosophy*, constituting the first of the two volumes of *An Entire Body of Philosophy According to the Principles of the Famous Renate Descartes* (London, 1694)—this last edition, being a coffee-table book, was no longer explicitly intended for students. Works such as these allow one to see how Cartesian philosophy was taught and disseminated in late seventeenth-century England.

33. Antoine Le Grand, *Entire Body of Philosophy* I, 347, col. b.

immovable *Mind* and *Will*, of doing those things which *Reason commands*, not suffering our *Passions* and corrupt *Inclinations* to lead us aside." And the third is "that we lay down as unmovable *Ground* and *Principle*, that nothing besides our own *Thoughts* is in our *Power*." Le Grand concludes "that the *Natural Happiness* of *Man* is nothing else but that *Tranquility* or *Joy* of *Mind*, which springs from his Possession or Enjoyment of the *Highest Good*."[34]

Given these ethical foundations, Le Grand examines how to avoid the excesses and ill use of the passions, but first he argues, against the Stoics and for the Cartesian view, that the passions or affections "are good and contribute to the Perfection of *Human Life*," when the objects of the passions are lawful and the passions proportionate to their objects.[35] According to Le Grand, the passions do not lead humans to vice; they are useful as long as they "are subject to the command and guidance of *Reason* and proportion'd to their *objects* and *end*; which only takes place when those things are *Loved* that ought to be *Loved* and when such *Objects* are loved in a higher degree, which because of their greater worth deserve more of our *Love*."[36] In the chapter on the governance of the passions and the remedies for them, he discusses generosity as another general remedy: it is "the *Key* to all *Vertue*," and "a powerful means to subdue and moderate our *Affections*." Since generosity consists in valuing and esteeming ourselves to the utmost of our worth, we can attain felicity if we find in ourselves a constant resolution to make good use of our will, that is, to undertake what we judge to be best, given that nothing properly belongs to ourselves other than how we dispose of our will and choice.[37] Still, Le Grand does not end his discussion of remedies with generosity. He adds that "the most powerful *Antidote* against our *Affections* is the Love of GOD."[38] While he

---

34. Le Grand, *Entire Body of Philosophy* I, 353, col. b.
35. Le Grand, *Entire Body of Philosophy* I, 368, col. a. While Descartes's views on happiness look very much like Christianized or Neo-Stoicism, Descartes's views on the passions offer a clear contrast with Neo-Stoicism. For the latter, see Guillaume Du Vair, *La Philosophie morale des Stoïques* (Paris, 1641). Du Vair's work started as a preface to his translation of Epictetus's *Enchiridion*, published in 1600, and was itself translated several times into English.
36. Le Grand, *Entire Body of Philosophy* I, 368, col. b.
37. Le Grand, *Entire Body of Philosophy* I, 376, col. a. These, of course, are from the letters to Elisabeth.
38. Le Grand, *Entire Body of Philosophy* I, 376, col. a–b.

cannot refer to *Passions of the Soul* for this, he does think it is Descartes's view and concludes by referring his reader to the 35th Epistle of volume 1 of Descartes's correspondence, which, of course, is the *Dissertation on Love*, that is, the letter to Chanut of February 1, 1647, that makes up much of the third part of Descartes's *Ethics*.

In the letter to Chanut, Descartes is answering questions from Queen Christina such as "What is love?" and "Does the natural light alone teach us to love God?"[39] In the former question, Descartes distinguishes between intellectual or rational love and love as a passion involving the body. According to him, intellectual love "is nothing other than when our soul perceives some present or absent good it judges to be suitable for itself, it attaches itself to it willingly."[40] But he asserts that in this life, when the soul is joined to the body, rational love is accompanied by sensual or sensitive love: "Ordinarily, these two loves occur together; for there is such a connection between them that, when the soul judges an object to be worthy of it, it immediately disposes the heart toward the motions exciting the passion of love; and when the heart finds itself thus disposed by other causes, it makes the soul imagine loveable qualities in objects."[41] This intermingling of the two loves makes it difficult for natural light by itself to be teaching us to love God; in this life the love of God cannot be purely intellectual, but must also have a sensitive aspect: "It would have to pass through the imagination in order to come from the understanding into the senses."[42] Only then can knowledge of God through the natural light be said to properly teach us to love God. Descartes produces a number of powerful objections against the possibility of love of God in this life: God's attributes are beyond us and nothing about God can be visualized by the imagination. But he sketches a way for us to attain the love of God by having our mind represent to itself the truths that excite in us the love of God. We should consider that he is a mind, that our soul's nature resembles his; we should take account of the infinity of his power, the extent of his providence, etc. This allows us to communicate this love to the imaginative faculty: "We can imagine our love itself, which consists in wanting to unite ourselves with some object.

---

39. Respectively, Descartes, *Ethice*, chap. 3.1 and 3.2.
40. AT IV, 602.
41. AT IV, 603.
42. AT IV, 607.

With respect to God this is to consider ourselves as a very small part of the immensity of things he has created; [...] and the idea of this union alone suffices to excite the heat around the heart and cause a very violent passion."[43] Descartes concludes that "our love for God must be without comparison the greatest and most perfect of all."[44] This final Cartesian doctrine introduces a theocentric element in Cartesian ethics but it also causes it to be a bit less intellectualist as well, since it requires the body and imagination to play a significant role.

---

43. AT IV, 610.
44. AT IV, 613.

NOTES ON THE EDITION AND TRANSLATION

Descartes's *Ethice* is an edition by an anonymous editor of posthumously published letters written by Descartes and the very late published treatise *Passions of the Soul*. All these materials were translated from their original French language into Latin, compiled, ordered, and abridged to produce an exemplary seventeenth-century treatise on ethics, or moral philosophy. Given that these texts were originally in French, it made little sense to translate the Latin edition. Thus, I translated Descartes's original French writings and indicated any deviations by the anonymous editor. I placed significant departures from Descartes's text—usually paraphrases of various paragraphs or sentences used as transitions—in angle brackets < >; interventions on my part are placed in square brackets [ ]. I indicate in the footnotes when a sentence was given out of order. I also indicate any missing text in the anonymous editor's edition, especially when the deletion occurs between sentences the editor chooses to display; short phrases or sentences are restored to the text and placed within curly brackets { }. The editor usually removes the salutation and closing of any letter, as well as extraneous materials; I do not normally indicate when these are missing.

I provide an appendix of relevant materials not given by the anonymous editor, such as Part 3 of Descartes's *Discourse on Method*, on the "provisional" morals, and a portion of the preface to the French-language edition of Descartes's *Principles of Philosophy* on the "tree" of philosophy. I also provide portions of other letters to illuminate the context for the correspondence used by the anonymous editor: objections and replies to the provisional morals; Princess Elisabeth's side of her correspondence with Descartes (unavailable to the editor); letters between Chanut and Descartes; and some items setting the context for the *Passions of the Soul*.

Translation is always difficult. It is especially so when dealing with texts, in different languages, written more than 300 years ago, and purporting to be about the same text. It is not as if one is always satisfied with one's solution to an issue in translation. And when one is dealing with a text such as the *Passions of the Soul* (*Les passions de l'âme*, *Passiones animae*), the problems are further aggravated. I think I can differentiate some of the subtle nuances among various concepts (in English, French, and Latin) such as abhorrence, antipathy, aversion, contempt, disdain, disgust, dislike, distaste, hatred, horror, loathing, repulsion, and revulsion. But perhaps not. In any case, there are hard choices to be made. I would like to discuss two such choices, from among many.

Descartes has six primitive passions: *admiration, amour, haine, désir, joie,* and *tristesse*. *Passiones animae* (Amsterdam, 1650) lists them as *admiratione, amor, odium, cupiditatis, laetitia,* and *tristitia*. *Passions of the Soul* (London, 1650)[1] lists them as admiration, love, hatred, desire, joy, and sadness. While all this looks straightforward, there is a problem with the first primitive passion, *admiration/admiratione*. Descartes calls it "a surprise" of the soul, and indeed, the term starts out to mean "surprise." *Nihil admirari* means "to be surprised by nothing." Moreover, there are around a dozen occasions when Descartes says *j'admire* when he means "I am surprised."[2] You can see the concept change over time to become, by the nineteenth century, the same as our "admire"—that is, "to feel respect and approval for someone or something," and leave behind the archaic form "to marvel at," which came from the Latin *admirari* "to regard with wonder," from *ad* + *mirari* "to be surprised, look with wonder at." The uneasy solution is to translate admiration with "wonder at," which connotes a surprise, especially because we still also say "wonder how" and "wonder why."

Another problematic concept is *la lâcheté*, which, as Descartes says, "is directly opposed to courage." The 1650 *Passions of the Soul* has no problem translating *la lâcheté* with "cowardice," but that seems too strong a term, when Descartes goes on to discuss the good function (*usage, usus*) of this

---

1. The fact that *Passions of the Soul* was translated into English within a year of its publication indicates the great interest in the topic. One could cite other works in English commenting on Descartes's *Passions*, including Walter Charleton's *Natural History of the Passions* (London, 1674). In his Prefatory Epistle to the work, Charleton quotes the whole of Descartes's article 47, so as to refute its physiology of the pineal gland at length. However, he ends the Epistle by saying: "In the description of many of the *Passions* . . . I have interwoven some threds taken from the webbs of those three excellent Men, *Gassendus, Des Cartes,* and our *Mr. Hobbes*; who have all written most judiciously of that obstruse theme." See as well the curious work of the French ex-Jesuit Peter Berault, *Logick, or the Key of the Sciences* (London, 1690), Part II: *Moral Science or the Way to be Happy,* 206–24.

2. For example, "j'admire que vos deux lettres aient pu s'entresuivre de si près" (AT I, 559), "J'admire que le traité . . . ait trouvé des défenseurs" (AT II, 2), "J'admire votre bonté, et pardonnez-moi si j'ajoute votre crédulité" (AT II, 26), "J'admire derechef que vous me mandiez" (AT II, 28).

passion. Some resolve the tension with "timidity," which seems a bit too weak to be the opposite of courage. The 1650 *Passiones animae* uses *pusillanimitas* (as does *Ethice*); "pusillanimity" seems just right. Of course, all three are synonyms of each other.

One final comment might be in order about translating *vouloir* (*velle*). It is often given as "to will," which I find awkward in most settings. In addition, saying that the passions incite us "to will" something tends to suggest that our will is more determined than inclined by the passions. Rendering *vouloir* as "to want" often yields the most natural-sounding English translation but can suggest desire (which is a passion), rather than an inclination of the will. The word "wish" might avoid these two implications, but it tends to obscure the fact that Descartes is describing the effect of the passions on the faculty of the will. Not finding any easy solution, I decided on "want" for *vouloir* in most cases. I hope to have been generally consistent, or at least not to have used "desire" on any such occasions.

ABBREVIATIONS

AT
: *Oeuvres de Descartes,* ed. by Charles Adam and Paul Tannery, 11 vols. (2nd edition, Paris: Vrin, 1969). Page number references to this edition are given in the margins

Clerselier
: *Lettres de Mr Descartes,* ed. Claude Clerselier, 3 vols. (Paris, 1657–1667)

Epistolae
: *Renati Descartes Epistolae,* [trans. Johannes de Raey], 2 vols. (Amsterdam and London, 1668)

< >
: Denotes departures or paraphrases from Descartes's text by the original editor

{ }
: Denotes short phrases or sentences omitted by the original editor and restored to the text by the present editor

[ ]
: Denotes interventions by the present editor

Chapter I

The Greatest Good[1]

The goodness of each thing can be considered in itself, without relating it to anything else. In this sense {it is evident that} God is the supreme good {since he is incomparably more perfect than creatures}. But it can also be related to us, and in that sense, I see nothing we should esteem good, except what belongs to us in some way, and which is such that it is a perfection for us to have it. {The ancient philosophers, not being enlightened by the light of faith, knew nothing of supernatural beatitude and considered only the goods we could possess in this life; thus, it was among these that they sought to determine which one was the highest, that is, the principal and greatest one.} But, in order that I might determine this, I think we must consider goods concerning us as either those we possess, or as those we have the power to acquire. And given that, it seems to me that the supreme good of all people together is a heap or collection of all the goods, as much of the soul as of the body and fortune, that could exist in people; but the supreme good of each individual is something entirely different and consists only in a firm will to do well and in the contentment it produces.[2] {The reason for this is that I can observe no other good which seems as great to me and entirely within each person's power.} <It is a most perfect good in this life and everyone possesses it.> For the goods of the body and fortune do not depend absolutely on us; and those of the soul all relate to two main things, one of which is *knowing* what is good and the other *willing* it; but knowledge is often beyond our capacities; that is why there remains only our will of which we have absolute control. And I do not see how it would be possible to use it better than by always having a firm and constant resolution to do exactly those things we judge to be the best, and to use all the power of our minds to know them well. It is in this alone that consist all the virtues; it is this alone which, properly speaking,

V, 82

83

---

1. From Descartes to Christina (November 20, 1647), AT V, 82–85, Clerselier/*Epistolae* Letter 1.
2. The Latin version in *Epistolae* and in *Ethice* has "tranquility of soul (*animi tranquillitas*)," instead of "contentment (*contentement*)."

deserves praise and glory. {Finally, it is from this alone that the greatest and most solid contentment in life always results. Thus, I find the supreme good to consist in this.}

And in that way, I believe I can reconcile the two most contrary and most famous views of the ancients, namely Zeno's, who placed the good in virtue or honor, and Epicurus's, who placed it in contentment, to which he gave the name of pleasure. As all vices come only from the uncertainty and weakness resulting from ignorance and leading to repentance, likewise virtue consists only in the resolution and vigor <of the mind> leading us to do things we believe to be good, provided that this vigor does not come from stubbornness, but from the knowledge that we examined the things as much as is morally within our power. {And, although what we then go on to do might be bad, we are nevertheless sure of doing our duty; whereas, if we perform some virtuous action but intend to do wrong, or neglect trying to understand its nature, we do not act as a virtuous person.} As for honor and praise,[3] it does not seem to me that we have reason to praise anything but the above virtue. All other goods deserve only to be esteemed and not to be honored or praised, except insofar as we suppose them to be acquired or obtained by the good use of free will. For honor and praise are a kind of reward, and only what depends on the will is subject to reward or punishment.

{It still remains for me here to prove that the proper use of free will produces the greatest and most solid contentment in life; this does not seem difficult, since, in carefully considering} what sensual delights or pleasure consist in {and generally all sorts of contentment we can have}, I observe first that all of them are entirely in the soul, even though many depend on the body—just as it is also the soul that sees, but through the intermediary of the eyes. Next, I observe that nothing can give contentment to the soul except the belief it has of possessing some good {and that often this belief is but a very confused representation in the soul. Further, the soul's union with the body is the reason it typically represents certain goods to itself as incomparably greater than they are}; but, if it knew their just value distinctly, its contentment would always be proportional to the greatness of the good from which it proceeded. The greatness of a good, where we are concerned, must not only be measured by the value in which it consists, but primarily by the way it is related to us. {In addition, free will is in itself

---

3. Omitted: they are often attributed to the other goods of fortune; but, because I am sure your Majesty values her virtue more than her crown, I will not fear saying here that

the most noble thing that can be in us, insofar as} its proper usage is the greatest of all our goods and in some way makes us like God.

The Happy Life[4]

<I first note that> there is a difference between fortune and bliss, in that fortune depends only on things outside of us; as a result, we are thought more fortunate than wise if some good comes to us that we did not procure for ourselves; but it seems to me that bliss consists in a perfect contentment[5] of mind and an inner satisfaction not commonly possessed by those most favored by fortune, and which the wise acquire without it. Thus, to live happily, to live in bliss, is nothing more than to have a perfectly content and satisfied mind. <With respect to what makes a life happy,>[6] there are two kinds of such things: namely, those that depend on us, like virtue and wisdom, and those that do not, like honors, riches, and health. For it is certain that a person of good birth who is not ill, who lacks nothing, and who is also as wise and as virtuous as someone else who is poor, unhealthy, and deformed, can enjoy a more perfect contentment than the latter. However, just as a small vessel can be as full as a larger one, although it contains less liquid, {taking each person's contentment as the fullness and satisfaction of all his desires regulated according to reason,} I do not doubt that the poorest people, least blessed by fortune or nature, can be entirely content and satisfied, just as much as others, even though they do not enjoy as many goods. {And only this kind of contentment is in question here; for, since the other is not at all in our power, to seek it would be superfluous.} <But it is necessary that these three Rules of morality be observed.>[7]

The first is that he should {always try to use his mind, as well as he can, to} know what he should or should not do in all circumstances of life.

---

4. From Descartes to Elisabeth (August 4, 1645), AT IV, 264–66, Clerselier/*Epistolae* Letter 4, and (September 1, 1645), AT IV, 281–87, Clerselier/*Epistolae* Letter 6.
5. Again, and below, *Epistolae* and *Ethice* have *tranquillitate* instead of *contentement*.
6. Original text: Next let us consider what *makes a life happy*, that is, what are the things that can give us this supreme contentment. I observe that
7. Original text: Now, it seems to me that each person can make himself content by himself without expecting anything else, provided only that he observes three things, to which are related the three rules of morality I put forward in the *Discourse on Method* [AT VI, 22–27].

The second is that he should have a firm and constant resolution to carry out everything reason will counsel him without being diverted by his passions or appetites. <And this is the *only thing* I believe should be taken for virtue, even though others>[8] divided it into several species to which they gave various names, because of the various objects to which it extends.[9]

The third is that he should consider that while he guides himself thus, as much as he can, according to reason, all the goods he does not possess are also one and all entirely outside his power. In this way he accustoms himself not to desire them; for nothing but desire and regret or repentance can prevent our being content. {But if we always do everything our reason dictates to us, we will never have any subject for regret, even if events show us afterward that we were mistaken, because being mistaken is not through our own fault. We do not desire to have, for example, more arms or more tongues than we have, but we do desire to have more health or more riches. The reason for this is only that we imagine the latter things can be acquired by our conduct, or are due to our nature, but it is not the same for the former; we can rid ourselves of that opinion by considering that, since we have always followed the advice of our reason, we omitted nothing that was in our power, and that sickness and misfortune are no less natural to humans than prosperity and health.} Moreover, not every kind of desire is incompatible with happiness; only those accompanied by impatience and sadness are so. It is also not necessary that our reason should not be mistaken; it is sufficient if our conscience testifies that we never lacked resolution and virtue for carrying out everything we judged to be the best. Thus, virtue alone <(which, if it is unenlightened by the understanding, is the least solid, but, if the right use of reason is made, is the sweetest)>[10] is sufficient to make us content in this life.

[11]When I spoke of a happiness that depends entirely on our free will,[12] it should be understood to apply only to those who have the free use of

---

8. Original text: And it is the firmness of this resolution that I believe should be taken for virtue, even though I do not know that anyone ever explained it in this way. Instead, they
9. In the margin of Descartes, *Ethics*: *We recognize nothing else as virtue.*
10. The parenthetical is a summary of what Descartes asserts in the next paragraph.
11. From Descartes to Elisabeth (September 1, 1645), AT IV, 281–87, Clerselier/*Epistolae* Letter 6.
12. Omitted: and which all people can acquire without assistance from elsewhere, you remark very well [see Elisabeth to Descartes (August 16 [1645]), AT IV, 269] that there are illnesses which take away the power of reasoning and with it the power of enjoying the satisfaction proper to a rational mind. This tells me that what I said in general about all people,

their reason and who also know the road that must be followed to reach such beatitude. For often bodily indisposition prevents the will from being free, <and some people wish to make themselves happy, but they do not understand how it can be done >. {This happens too when we sleep; for the world's most philosophical person could not prevent himself from having bad dreams when his temperament so disposes him. However, experience shows that if we often had a particular thought when our mind was at liberty, it returns later, whatever indisposition the body may have. Thus, I can say that my dreams never represent anything unpleasant to me, and there is no doubt that it is a great advantage to have long become accustomed to reject sad thoughts. But we cannot absolutely answer for ourselves except when we are ourselves, and it is a lesser thing to lose one's life than to lose the use of one's reason; for even without the teachings of faith, natural philosophy alone makes us hope that our soul will be in a happier state after death than the one it is in at present, and makes it fear nothing more unpleasant than being attached to a body that completely takes away its freedom.}

As for the other indispositions that do not completely trouble the senses but only alter the humors and make us unusually inclined to sadness, or anger, or some other passion, these no doubt cause pain, but they can be overcome; moreover, the more difficult they are to conquer, the greater the satisfaction the soul can derive from this. {I believe the same is true of all external impediments, such as the brilliance of high birth, the adulation of the Court, the adversities of fortune, as well as great wealth, which commonly does more than misfortune to prevent us from playing the role of a philosopher. For when we receive everything we want, we forget to think of ourselves; and afterward, when fortune changes, we are more surprised the more we trusted in it. In the end, we can say in general that nothing can completely take away our means of making ourselves happy as long as our reason is not troubled;} and it is not always the things that seem the most unpleasant that do the most harm.

{But in order to know exactly how much each thing can contribute to our contentment, we must consider what are the causes that produce it; and this is also one of the principal items of knowledge that can serve to facilitate the use of virtue, for} all the actions of our soul that enable us to acquire some perfection are virtuous, and all our contentment consists only in our internal awareness that we have some perfection. Thus, we cannot ever practice any virtue (that is, do what our reason persuades us we should do) without receiving satisfaction and pleasure from this. But there are two kinds of pleasures: those belonging to the mind alone, and those belonging to {the person, that is, to} the mind insofar as it is united to the body. These latter ones, presenting themselves confusedly to the imagination, often appear much greater than they are, especially before we possess them; and this is the source of all evils and all errors in life. {For, according to the rule of reason, each pleasure should be measured by the magnitude of the perfection producing it; it is thus that we measure those whose causes are clearly known to us.} But often passion makes us believe certain things much better and more desirable than they are; then, when we have taken much pain to acquire them, and in the meanwhile lost the occasion to possess other more genuine goods, possession of them allows us to know their defects; from this arises disdain, regret, and remorse. This is why the true function of reason is to examine the just value of all the goods {whose acquisition seems to depend in some way on our conduct, in order that we never fail to use all our efforts in trying to procure for ourselves those that are in fact the most desirable}. If fortune opposes our plans in this and prevents them from succeeding, we will have at least the satisfaction of never having lost anything through our fault and will still enjoy all the natural happiness whose acquisition was within our power. [. . .]

This is why we commonly blame pleasure, because we use the word to mean only the pleasures that frequently deceive us by their appearance and make us neglect other much more solid ones, but whose anticipation is not as great, such as the pleasures of the mind by itself commonly are. I say "commonly" because not all pleasures of the mind are praiseworthy, because they can be founded on some false opinion, such as the pleasure we take in slander, which is founded only on our thinking that we would be that much more esteemed to the extent others would be less so. {And they can also deceive us by their appearance, when some strong passion accompanies them, as can be seen in the pleasure ambition provides.}

But the main difference between the pleasures of the body and those of the mind consists in that, since the body is subject to perpetual change, and even its preservation and well-being depend on this change, all the pleasures proper to it last but a very short time, for they arise only from the acquisition of something useful to the body at the moment they are received, and cease as soon as it stops being useful to it. On the other hand, the pleasures of the soul can be as immortal as the soul itself, provided they have such a solid foundation that neither the knowledge of truth nor any false conviction can destroy them.

{Moreover, the true use of our reason in the conduct of life consists only in examining and considering without passion the value of all the perfections, both of the body and of the mind, that can be acquired by our conduct, so that since we are commonly obliged to deprive ourselves of some of them in order to acquire others, we will always choose the better ones.} And because the pleasures of the body are lesser, it can be said in general that there is a way to become happy without them. However, I am not of the opinion that they should be entirely disdained, nor even that we must exempt ourselves from having passions. It is enough to make them subject to reason; and once they are thus tamed, they are sometimes more useful to the extent that they tend more toward excess.

How the Understanding Is Confirmed in Its Knowledge That the Greatest Good Lies in the Actions of Life[13]

There can only be two things required to always be disposed to judge well: one is *knowledge* of the truth and the other is the *habit* allowing us to remember and acquiesce to this knowledge whenever the occasion requires it. But because only God knows all things perfectly, we need to content ourselves with knowing the ones most useful to us.

The *first* and principal one of these is that there is a God on whom all things depend {whose perfections are infinite, whose power is immense, and whose decrees are infallible}. For this teaches us to accept favorably the things happening to us, as expressly sent to us by God. {And because the true object of love is perfection, when we elevate our minds to consider him as he is, we find ourselves naturally so inclined to love him that we even derive joy from our afflictions, by thinking that his will is performed by our receiving them.}

The second thing we must know is the nature of our soul, insofar as it subsists without the body, {is much nobler than it,} and is capable of enjoying an infinity of contentment {not to be found in this life}. For this

---

13. From Descartes to Elisabeth (September 15, 1645), AT IV, 291–96, Clerselier/*Epistolae* Letter 7.

prevents us from fearing death, and so detaches our affections from the things of this world that we regard with nothing but scorn whatever is in the power of fortune.

<The third is> that we judge the works of God with dignity and have a vast idea of the extent of the universe.[14] For if we conceive that beyond the heavens there is nothing but imaginary spaces, and all the heavens are made only for the service of the earth, and the earth only for man, we will be inclined to think that this earth is our principal domain and this life is our best. {And instead of understanding the perfections that are truly in us, we would attribute to other creatures some imperfections they do not have, to elevate ourselves above them, and} we would become so absurdly presumptuous as to wish to belong to God's council and take charge of the conduct of the world along with him; this will cause us an infinity of useless anxieties and troubles.}

[15]<The fourth is that> we must think that we could not subsist alone and that we are, in fact, one of the parts of the universe, and more specifically one of the parts of this earth, this State, this society, and this family to which we are joined by our domicile, our faith, and our birth. And we must always prefer the interests of the whole, of which we are a part, to those of our own person individually—though with measure and discretion, for we would be wrong to expose ourselves to a great evil to procure only a slight good for our parents or our country; and if someone were of greater value, by himself, than the rest of his town, he would have no reason to want to waste himself to save it. But if someone related everything to himself, {he would not fear greatly harming others when he thought he could derive some slight service to himself; and} he would have no true friendship, no faithfulness, and in general no virtue. Instead, by considering ourselves as part of the public, we take pleasure in doing good to the whole world {and even do not fear endangering our lives in the service of others when the occasion presents itself; indeed, we would even be willing to lose our souls, if it is possible, in order to save others. And thus, this

---

14. Original text: For this, it may also be very useful that we judge the works of God with dignity and have a vast idea of the extent of the universe, such as I tried to have people conceive in book III of my *Principles*.

15. Omitted: After thus acknowledging God's goodness, our souls' immortality and the universe's immensity, there is still another truth the knowledge of which seems most useful, that is, even though each of us is a person distinct from others, whose interests are consequently in some way distinct from those of the rest of the world,

consideration is the source and origin of all the most heroic actions done by people}. As for those who risk death from vanity because they hope to be praised for it, or through stupidity, because they do not apprehend the danger, I believe such people are more pitiful than admirable. But when someone risks death because he believes it is his duty, or when he suffers some other harm, because it brings some good to others, although he perhaps considers it without reflecting that he does it because he owes more to the public, of which he is a part, than to himself as an individual, he still acts, however, in virtue of the consideration which is confusedly in his thought. {We are naturally led to think in this way once we know and love God as we should; for then, abandoning ourselves completely to his will, we strip ourselves of our own interests, and have no other passion than to do what we think pleasing to God.} As a result, we acquire satisfaction and contentment of mind incomparably more valuable than all the passing joys that depend on the senses.

<Fifth>, we must also know several truths I mentioned before[16]: namely, that all our passions represent to us the goods, to whose pursuit they incite us, as being much greater than they truly are; and that the pleasures of the body are never as lasting as those of the soul {or as great when we possess them, as they appear when we hope for them}. We must carefully make note of this, so that when we feel ourselves moved by some passion, we suspend our judgment until it is appeased, and do not let ourselves be deceived by the false appearance {of the goods of this world}.

I do not have anything more to add, except that we must also examine individually all the customs of places in which we live, to understand to what extent they must be followed. And even though we cannot have certain demonstrations of everything, we must still take sides, and embrace the opinions that seem the most probable to us {concerning all the things of common use, so that when we need to act, we are never irresolute}; for doubt causes regret and remorse.

Moreover, I said before that besides knowledge of the truth, *habit* is also required in order to be disposed always to judge well. {For we cannot be continually attentive to the same thing. However clear and evident were the reasons that previously persuaded us of some truth, we can

---

16. Original text: In addition to these truths regarding all our actions in general, we also need to know several others regarding each one of them more specifically. The main one of these, it seems to me, are those I mentioned in my last letter [Descartes to Elisabeth (September 1, 1645), AT IV, 285]:

later be deterred from believing it by some false appearances, unless we so imprinted it on our minds by long and frequent meditation that it became a settled habit in us.} In this sense the Scholastics are right to say that virtues are habits; for in fact, we hardly fail by lacking theoretical knowledge of what we should do, but by lacking practical knowledge, that is, by lacking a firm habit of believing it.

Whether in This Life There Are More Goods Than Evils[17]

When we consider the idea of the good that serves as a rule for our actions, we take it to have all the perfection that can be in the thing we call good and compare it to a straight line, the only one from among an infinity of curved lines, to which we compare the evils. It is in this sense that philosophers have the habit of saying that *the good arises from the whole cause, the evil from some deficiency*.[18] But, when we consider the goods and evils that can be in one and the same thing, to understand how we are to value it, as I did when I spoke of the value we should make of this life, we take the good to be anything found in it from which we might receive some advantage, and we call evil only that from which we might receive some disadvantage; for we do not count the other defects that might be there. {Thus, when one offers employment to someone, he considers, on the one hand, the honor and the profit that he might expect from it as goods, and, on the other hand, the trouble, the risk, the loss of time, and such other things, as evils; and comparing these evils with these goods, according to whether he finds these more or less great than those, he accepts or rejects the employment. Now, what made me say,} in this sense, that there are always more goods than evils in this life is the little importance I believe we should give to all the things outside of us, and that do not depend on our free will, compared to those that do depend on it, which we can always make good when we truly know how to use them. And, by their means, we can prevent all the evils that come from elsewhere, however great they might be, from

---

17. From Descartes to Elisabeth [January 1646], AT IV, 354–56, Clerselier/*Epistolae* Letter 10.

18. A Scholastic maxim that can be found in Thomas Aquinas's *Summa* Theologiae (I.2, q. 18, Art. 4), quoting with approbation pseudo-Dionysus, *On the Divine Names*, chap. 4, and elsewhere.

entering any further into our souls than does the sadness provoked by actors when they represent before us some very tragic action; but I admit that we must be strongly philosophical to come to this point. And however I also believe that even those who allow themselves to be most carried away by their passions still judge, internally, that there are more goods than evils in this life, even though they do not themselves perceive them; for, although they sometimes call death to their rescue when they feel great pain, it is only in order that it helps them to carry their burden, as it is in the fable,[19] and they do not want to lose their lives on this account; or, if there are some who do want to lose it, and who kill themselves, it is by an error in their understanding, and not by a well-reasoned judgment, nor by an opinion that nature imprinted in them, as is the opinion which has us prefer the goods of this life to its evils.

356

Free Will[20]

Indifference seems to me, strictly speaking, to signify that state in which the will finds itself when it is not led by the knowledge of what is true or what is good to follow one side rather than the other; {I was taking it} in this sense, {when I said that} the lowest degree of freedom consists in being able to determine ourselves to things to which we are wholly indifferent. But perhaps others mean by indifference the positive faculty we have of determining ourselves to one or the other of two contraries, that is, of pursuing or fleeing, of affirming or denying. {I did not deny that} this positive faculty is in the will. {Indeed, I think it is there, not only whenever it is not at all led by the weight of any evident reason to one side rather than to another,} and it is even involved in all the other actions of the will, <so that the will is never determined without using that faculty>. Thus, when {a very evident} reason leads us to something, even though, morally speaking, it is difficult

III, 378

379

---

19. A reference to fable 78 by Aesop, "The Old Man and Death," retold by Jean de la Fontaigne in "La Mort et le Bûcheron."

20. Descartes to Mersenne (May 27, 1641), AT III, 378–80, Clerselier/*Epistolae* Letter 112 and AT III, 704–6. There is a slightly different Latin version of this letter, given as Descartes to [Mesland?] [February 9, 1645?], AT IV, 173–75. This Latin version comes from a manuscript copy that would not have been available to the original editor (who followed *Epistolae* Letter 112). One can find an English translation of the new Latin version in John Cottingham et al., *The Philosophical Writings of Descartes*, Vol. III (Cambridge: Cambridge University Press, 1991), 244–46.

for us to do the contrary, nevertheless, speaking absolutely, we can. For we are always free to prevent ourselves from pursuing a good most clearly known to us or from admitting an evident truth, as long as we think it good to test the freedom of our will in this way.

Further, it must be observed that freedom can be considered in the actions of the will either before they are accomplished or while they are being accomplished.

380 It is certain that considered in the actions of the will before they are accomplished, freedom implies indifference understood in the second sense, but not in the first. That is, before our will is determined {it is always free, or} has the power of choosing one or the other of two opposite things. But in truth, it is not always indifferent; on the contrary, we never deliberate except to rid ourselves of this state in which we do not know which side to take, or to prevent ourselves from falling into it. When we oppose our own judgment to orders received from others, we tell ourselves we are freer when we do what no one else ordered us to do, and when we follow our own judgment, than when we do what is ordered of us. However, we cannot speak in the same way when we oppose our own judgment and our own knowledge to one another, and say we are freer to do those things that seem to us neither good nor bad, or in which we see as many arguments for good as for bad, than when we are to do those things in which we see much more good than bad. For, greater freedom consists either in a greater facility of self-determination or in a greater use of that positive power we have to follow the worse while seeing the better. And if we follow the side where we see more good, we determine ourselves more easily. But if we fol-

381 low the opposite side, we make more use of our positive power. And thus, we can always act more freely in the things in which we see more good than bad, than in the things we call indifferent. In this sense also we can say that we do less freely the things we are ordered to do by others that we would otherwise not do ourselves, than those we were not ordered to do. For the judgment that they are difficult to do is opposed to the judgment that it is good to do what one is ordered to do, and the more these two judgments move us equally, the more they confer on us indifference taken in the sense I first explained it, that is, which places the will in a state of not knowing to what it should be determined.

Now, considered in the actions of the will while they are being accomplished, freedom does not contain any indifference, in whatever sense we take it, since what is done cannot remain undone once it is done. But freedom consists only in the facility of execution, which, to the extent it increases, freedom also increases; and thus free, spontaneous, and voluntary are all one and the same thing. [21]As for animals {lacking reason}, it is evident they are not free, because they do not have this positive power of self-determination. But freedom in them is a pure negation, of not being forced or constrained.

IV, 117

Nothing prevented me from speaking of the freedom we have to follow the good or bad <even with respect to Predestination>, except that I wanted to avoid theology here; [22]but in fact theologians distinguish in God an absolute and independent volition, by which he wills that all things happen as they do, and another relative volition, that relates to the merit or demerit of people, by which he wills that we obey his laws. [23]In thinking only of ourselves we cannot help regarding our free will as independent; but when we think of God's infinite power, we cannot help believing that all things depend on him {and that consequently our free will is not exempt from this}. <For it implies a contradiction that he is infinite and that there is something which does not depend on him.>[24]

IV, 354

IV, 332

---

21. From Descartes to [Mesland] [May 2, 1644?], IV, 117, Clerselier/*Epistolae* Letter 115.
22. From Descartes to Elisabeth [January 1646], AT IV, 354, Clerselier/*Epistolae* Letter 10.
23. From Descartes to Elisabeth (November 3, 1645), AT IV, 332 Clerselier/*Epistolae* Letter 7.
24. Original sentence: For it implies a contradiction to say that God created human beings of such a nature that the actions of their will do not depend on his, because it is the same as saying that his power is altogether finite and infinite: finite, since there is something that does not depend on it; and infinite, since he was able to create that independent thing.

Chapter II

The Passions in General[1]

[2]The philosophers generally call whatever happens or is made to happen a *passion* with respect to the subject to which it happens, and an action in respect to the subject that makes it happen. Thus, although the agent and the patient are often very different, the action and the passion are still the same thing, with two different names in view of the two different subjects to which it may be ascribed. [3]Accordingly, I also consider that we do not observe the existence of any subject acting more immediately upon our soul than the body to which it is joined, and we must consequently believe that what is a passion in the soul is usually an action in the body. Thus, there is no better means of arriving at a knowledge of our passions than by examining the difference between the soul and the body, in order to know to which of the two we should attribute each of the functions within us. [4]As to this, we will not find much difficulty if we realize that everything we experience as being in us, and that we also see able to exist in wholly inanimate bodies, must be attributed to our bodies alone. In contrast, everything in us that we cannot in any way conceive as possibly pertaining to a body must be attributed to our soul. [5]Thus, since we cannot conceive of the body as thinking in any way, we have reason to believe that every kind of thought existing in us belongs to the soul. And since we do not doubt that there are inanimate bodies able to move in as many, or in more, different ways than ours, and have as much heat or more—what experience shows us in a flame, which has much more heat and motion on its own than any of our limbs—we must believe that all the heat and all

---

1. From AT XI, 327–70. Original Subtitle: The Passions in General and Occasionally the Whole Nature of Man.
2. From Art. 1. *Whatever is a passion with respect to a given subject is always an action in some other respect.*
3. Art 2. *To understand the passions of the soul, the functions of the soul must be distinguished from those of the body.*
4. Art. 3. *What rule we must follow to bring about this result.*
5. Art. 4. *The heat and motion of the limbs proceed from the body, and thoughts from the soul.*

the motions within us pertain only to the body, inasmuch as they do not at all depend on thought. ⁶In this way we will avoid a very considerable error into which many have fallen, so much so that I believe this is the primary cause that has prevented our being able to explain satisfactorily as yet the passions and other things belonging to the soul. It consists in observing that <since> all dead bodies are deprived of heat and consequently of motion, <one can be persuaded that> the absence of soul was causing these motions and this heat to stop. Thus, without any justification it was believed that our natural heat and all the motions of our body depend upon the soul, although we ought on the contrary believe that the soul leaves us in death only because this heat ceases and the organs serving to move the body decay. ⁷{In order then to avoid this error, let us consider that death never comes to pass through the fault of the soul, but only because one of the principal parts of the body decays; and} let us judge that the body of a living man differs from that of a dead man, just as a watch or other automaton (that is, a machine that moves by itself) when it is wound up and contains in itself the corporeal principle of those motions for which it is designed along with all that is required for its action, differs from the same watch or other machine when it is broken and when the principle of its motion ceases to act.⁸

⁹All the motions we make without a contribution of our will (as frequently happens when we breathe, walk, eat, and in sum perform all those actions common to us and the animals), all these motions depend only on the conformation of our limbs and on the course that the spirits, excited by the heat of the heart, follow naturally in the brain, nerves, and muscles, just as the motions of a watch are performed simply by the strength of the springs and the form of the wheels. ¹⁰I demonstrate this here only with

---

6. Art. 5. *It is an error to believe that the soul supplies motion and heat to the body.*

7. Art. 6. *What difference there is between a living and a dead body.*

8. Omitted are Arts. 7. *A brief explanation of the parts of the body and of some of its functions*; 8. *What the principle of these functions is*; 9. *How the motion of the heart takes place*; 10. *How the animal spirits are produced in the brain*; 11. *How the motions of the muscles take place*; 12. *How external objects act on the sense organs*; 14. *Differences among the spirits can also make them take different courses*; and 15. *The causes of their diversity.*

9. From Art. 16. *How all the limbs may be moved by the objects of the senses and by the animal spirits without the aid of the soul.*

10. From Art. 13. *This action of external objects may lead the spirits in different ways into the muscles.*

an example. If someone quickly thrusts his hand against our eyes as if to strike us, even though we know him to be our friend, that he only does it in jest, and that he will take great care not to hurt us, we still have trouble preventing ourselves from closing our eyes. And this shows that it is not by the intervention of the soul that our eyes close, seeing that it happens against our will, which is the soul's only, or at least its principal, activity. Rather, it is because the machine of our body is so formed that the motion of the hand toward our eyes excites another motion in our brain, conducting the animal spirits into the muscles, causing the eyelids to close. <But we consign these things and many others to physics and anatomy, which concern the examination of the functions of the body.>

[11]There is nothing in us we ought to attribute to our soul except our thoughts, which are mainly of two sorts, one being the *actions* of the soul, and the other its *passions* <or *affects*>. Actions are our volitions,[12] since we find by experience that they proceed directly from our soul and appear to depend on it alone. On the other hand, we can generally call passions all the sorts of perceptions or knowledge found in us, since it is often not our soul that makes them what they are, and since the soul often receives them from the things represented by them. [13]Our volitions, again, are of two sorts. One set consists of those actions of the soul terminating in the soul itself, as when we will to love God, or generally apply our thoughts to some non-material object. The others are actions terminating in our body, as when, from the simple fact that we have a volition to take a walk, it follows that our legs move and that we walk. [14]Our *perceptions* are also of two sorts, and one of them has the soul as cause and the other the body. Those with the soul as cause are the perceptions of our acts of will and of all the imaginations or other thoughts that depend on them. For it is certain that we cannot will anything without by the same means perceiving that we will it. [15]When our soul applies itself to imagine something that does not exist, as when it represents to itself an enchanted palace or a chimera, and when it applies itself to consider something only intelligible and not imaginable, {for example, when considering its own nature}, the perceptions

---

11. From Art. 17. *What the functions of the soul are.*

12. Original text: Those I call its actions are all our volitions.

13. Art. 18. *Of the will.*

14. From Art. 19. *Of perception.*

15. Art. 20. *Of the imaginations and other thoughts formed by the soul.*

it has of these things depend principally on the act of will that causes it to perceive them. That is why we usually consider these as actions rather than passions. [16]Among the perceptions caused by the body, the largest part depends on the nerves, but there are also some that do not depend on them, that we call imaginings, as we do those I just spoke of, from which, however, they differ in that our will has no part in forming them. And this means that they cannot be placed among the number of the actions of the soul. They proceed only from the fact that when the spirits are agitated in different ways and meet with traces of different impressions that preceded them in the brain, they happen to take their course through certain pores rather than through others. Such are the illusions of our dreams and the daydreams we often have when awake, and when our thought wanders aimlessly without applying itself to anything of its own accord. But although some of these imaginings are passions of the soul, taking this word {in its more proper and more specific meaning, and since they may all be called thus if we take the word} in a more general sense, yet because they do not have such a notable and determinate cause as the perceptions the soul receives through the mediation of the nerves, they appear to be only a shadow and a picture—{before our being able to distinguish them very well, we must consider the difference prevailing among these others}.

[17]{It remains for us to observe here that all the same things that the soul perceives by the mediation of the nerves may also be represented by the fortuitous course of the animal spirits, without there being any difference except that the impressions coming into the brain through the nerves are usually more lively or definite than those excited there by the spirits. That is why I said[18] that the latter resemble the shadow or picture of the former.} It should also be observed that this picture is sometimes so similar to the thing it represents that we may be mistaken about the perceptions relating to external objects, or at least those relating to certain parts of our body, but we cannot be thus deceived about the passions, inasmuch as they are so close to, and so entirely within our soul, that it is impossible for it to feel them without their being actually such as it feels them to be. Thus, often when we are asleep, or sometimes even when we are awake,

---

16. Art. 21. *Of the imaginations that have the body only as cause.*
17. Art. 26. *The imaginations which depend on the fortuitous motions of the spirits may be just as truly passions as the perceptions that depend on the nerves.*
18. In Art. 21.

we imagine certain things so forcibly that we think we see them before us, or feel them in our body, although they do not exist at all; but although we may be asleep or dreaming, we cannot feel sad or moved by any other passion without its being very true that the soul actually has this passion within it. [19]All the other perceptions I did not yet explain come to the soul by the mediation of the nerves, and there is this difference between them, that we relate some of them to external objects that strike our senses, {others to our body or to some of its parts, and finally others to our soul}.

[20]{Those we relate to things outside ourselves, namely, to the objects of our senses, are caused, at least when our opinion is not false, by those objects, which, causing certain motions in the organs of the external senses, also excite certain motions in the brain through the mediation of the nerves, causing the soul to perceive them.} Thus, when we see the light of a torch and hear the sound of a bell, this light and this sound[21] that we relate [22]to our body or to some of its parts, <as we do,> are those we have of hunger, thirst, and other natural appetites, to which we may join pain, heat, and the other affections that we feel as if in our own limbs, and not as in external objects. {We may thus perceive at the same time, and by the mediation of the same nerves, the cold of our hand and the heat of the flame to which it is approaching, or, on the other hand, the heat of the hand and the cold of the air to which it is exposed, without there being any difference between the actions that cause us to feel the heat or the cold in our hand, and those that make us perceive what is outside us, except that, one of those actions following the other, we judge that the first is already in us, and the one that follows is not yet in us, but is in the object that causes it.} [23]{The perceptions we relate solely to the soul are those whose effects we feel as though they were in the soul itself, and for which we do not

---

19. Art. 22. *Of the difference that exists among the other perceptions.*
20. Art. 23. *Of the perceptions that we relate to external objects.*
21. Omitted: are two different actions, which, simply by fact that they excite two different motions in certain of our nerves, and by their means in the brain, give the soul two different sensations that we relate in such a way to the subjects that we suppose to be their cause, so that we think we see the torch itself and hear the bell, and not that we perceive only the motions proceeding from them.
22. Art. 24. *Of the perceptions that we relate to our body.*
23. Art. 25. *Of the perceptions we relate to our soul*; Art. 26. *The imaginations that depend on the fortuitous motions of the spirits may be just as truly passions as the perceptions that depend on the nerves* is omitted.

usually know any proximate cause to which we could relate them.} Such are the feelings of joy, anger, and other similar sensations, which are sometimes excited in us by the objects that move our nerves and sometimes also by other causes. But all our perceptions, both those we relate to external objects and those we relate to the different affections of our body, are truly passions in respect to our soul, {when we use this word in its most general sense; however, we are in the habit of restricting it to refer only to those related to the soul itself, and it is only the latter that I have undertaken to explain under the name of passions of the soul}.

[24]After having considered how the passions of the soul differ from all its other thoughts, I think we may define them generally as *perceptions, or sensations, or emotions of the soul that we relate especially to it, and that are caused, maintained, and fortified by some motion of the spirits.*

[25]{We also need to know that} although the soul is joined to the whole body, nevertheless there is in the body a certain part in which the soul exercises its functions more particularly than in all the others. {And it is usually believed that this part is the brain, or possibly the heart—the brain because the organs of sense are connected with it, and the heart because it appears as if we feel the passions in it. But after examining the matter with care,} it seems to me I clearly recognized that {the part of the body in which the soul exercises its functions immediately is not at all the heart, nor the whole of the brain, but merely the most inward of its parts, namely,} a certain very small gland situated in the middle of the brain's substance {and so suspended above the duct through which the animal spirits of its anterior cavities communicate with those of the posterior one, that the slightest motions taking place in it may alter very greatly the course of the spirits, and, reciprocally, that the smallest changes occurring in the course of the spirits can do much to change the motions of this gland}. [26]The reason that persuades me {that the soul cannot have any other location in all the body than this gland is that: I consider the fact} that the other parts of the brain are all double, just as we also have two eyes, two hands, two ears; and in sum all the organs of our external senses

---

24. Art. 27. *The definition of the passions of the soul.* Omitted are Art. 28. *Explanation of the first part of this definition,* 29. *Explanation of the second part,* and 30. *The soul is united conjointly to all the parts of the body.*

25. Art. 31. *There is a small gland in the brain in which the soul exercises its functions more particularly than in the other parts.*

26. Art. 32. *How we know that this gland is the principal seat of the soul*

are double; and inasmuch as we have but one solitary and simple thought of one particular thing at one and the same time, it must necessarily be the case that there is a place where the two images coming to us from the two eyes, or where the two other impressions proceeding through the double organs of the other senses, can unite before arriving in the soul, so that they do not represent to it two objects instead of one. {And it is easy to conceive that these images or other impressions might unite in this gland by the mediation of the spirits that fill the cavities of the brain. But there is no other place in the body where they can be thus united unless they are so in this gland.} [27]As to the opinion of those who think that the soul receives its passions in the heart, it is in no way to be considered, for it is based only on the fact that the passions cause us to feel some change taking place there. And it is easy to observe that this change is not felt in the heart except through the medium of a small nerve descending toward it from the brain, just as pain is felt in the foot by means of the nerves of the foot {and the stars are perceived as in the heavens by means of their light and the optic nerves. So, it is no more necessary that our soul should exercise its functions immediately in the heart in order to feel its passions there than it is necessary for the soul to be in the heavens in order to see the stars there}.[28] [29]The same impression that the presence of a scary object makes on the gland, and that causes fear in some people, can, in others, excite courage and confidence. This is because not all brains are constituted in the same way, and the same motion of the gland that excites fear in some, in others causes the spirits to enter the pores of the brain, conducting them partly into the nerves serving to move the hands for the purpose of self-defense, and partly into those agitating and driving the blood toward the heart in the manner required to produce the spirits proper for the continuance of defense, and to retain the will for it. [30]For, it is necessary to observe that the principal effect of all the passions in humans is that they incite and dispose their soul to want those things for which they prepare their body,

---

27. Art. 33. *The seat of the passions is not in the heart.*
28. Omitted are Art. 34. *How the soul and the body act on one another*; 35. *Example of the way in which the impressions of objects unite in the gland that is in the middle of the brain*; 36. *Example of the way in which the passions are excited in the soul*; 37. *How it seems that they are all caused by some motion of the spirits*; and 38. *Example of the motions of the body that accompany the passions and do not depend on the soul.*
29. Art. 39. *How one and the same cause may excite different passions in different people.*
30. Art. 40. *The principal effect of the passions.*

so that the feeling of fear incites it to want to take flight, that of courage to want to fight, and so on. [31]But the will is so free in its nature that it can never be constrained, {and of the two sorts of thoughts I distinguished in the soul—of which the first are its actions, that is, its volitions, and the other its passions, taking this word in its most general significance, which comprises all kinds of perceptions—the former are absolutely in its power, and can be changed only indirectly by the body, while on the other hand the latter depend absolutely on the actions that govern and direct them, and they can be altered only indirectly by the soul, except when it is itself their cause}. And the whole action of the soul consists in that merely by willing something, it causes the little gland to which it is closely united to move in the way required to produce the effect that relates to this volition.

[32]Thus, when the soul wants to recollect something, this volition causes the gland, by inclining successively to different sides, to thrust the spirits toward different parts of the brain until they come across that part where the traces left there by the object we want to recollect are found;[33] by this means they excite a special motion in the gland which represents the same object to the soul and causes it to know that this is what it wanted to remember. [34]{Thus, when we want to imagine something that we have never seen, this volition has the power of causing the gland to move in the manner required to drive the spirits toward those pores of the brain whose opening may represent this particular thing.} Thus also, when we want to apply our attention for some time to the consideration of a particular object, this volition holds the gland to the same side for that time. Thus finally, when we want to walk or to move our body in some special way, this volition causes the gland to thrust the spirits toward the muscles serving to bring about this result. [35]At the same time, it is not always the volition to excite in ourselves some motion or bring about

---

31. Art. 41. *What the power of the soul is regarding the body.*
32. Art. 42. *How we find in our memory the things we want to remember.*
33. Omitted: For these traces are nothing other than that the pores of the brain, by which the spirits have formerly followed their course because of the presence of this object, have by that means acquired a greater facility than others for being once more opened by the spirits coming toward them in the same way. So, these spirits, in coming into contact with these pores, enter into them more easily than into the others.
34. Art. 43. *How the soul can imagine, be attentive, and move the body.*
35. Art. 44. *Each volition is naturally united to some motion of the gland; but that, through effort or habit, it may be united to others.*

some other result that can excite the gland, for this changes according as nature or habit have united each motion of the gland differently to each particular thought. {Thus, for example, if we want to adjust our eyes to look at an object very far away, this volition causes the pupils to enlarge; and if we want to set them to look at an object very nearby, this volition causes them to contract. But if we think only of enlarging the pupil of the eye, we may indeed have the volition, but cannot enlarge it in that way, because nature has not joined the motion of the gland that serves to thrust forth the spirits toward the optic nerve in the manner required for enlarging or contracting the pupil with the volition to enlarge or diminish it, but with that of looking at objects that are far away or nearby. And when speaking we think only of the sense of what we want to say, which causes us to move the tongue and lips much more quickly and much better than if we thought of moving them in all the many ways required to utter the same words, inasmuch as the habit we acquired in learning to speak has caused us to join the action of the soul, which can move the tongue and lips through the mediation of the gland, with the meaning of the words that follow those motions, rather than with the motions themselves.} [36]Our passions as well cannot be directly excited or removed by the action of our will, but they can be so indirectly through the representation of things that are usually joined to the passions {that we want to have and are contrary to those we want to reject. Thus, in order to excite courage in ourselves and remove fear, it is not sufficient to have the will to do so, but we must also apply ourselves to consider the reasons, the objects, or the examples that persuade us that the peril is not great; that there is always more safety in defense than in flight; that we will have the glory and the joy of having vanquished, while we could expect nothing but regret and shame for having fled, and so on}. [37]There is a specific reason that prevents the soul from being able to alter or stop its passions at once, which led me to say, in defining them, that they are not only caused, but also maintained and strengthened, by some particular motion of the spirits. This reason is that they are nearly all accompanied by some disturbance[38] that takes place in the heart, and in consequence also in the

---

36. Art. 45. *What the power of the soul is regarding the passions.*
37. Art. 46. *The reason why the soul cannot wholly control its passions.*
38. What we are translating as "disturbance" here and below is *commotio* in *Ethice* and *émotion* in *Les Passions de l'Ame*. Descartes uses *émotion* for disturbances of both the soul and the body, but it would be odd to refer to "the emotion of the blood."

whole of the blood and the spirits, {so that until this disturbance has subsided, they remain present to our thought in the same way that sensible objects are present there while they are acting on our sense organs. And as the soul, in rendering itself very attentive to some other thing, may prevent itself from hearing a slight noise or feeling a slight pain, but cannot prevent itself in the same way from hearing thunder or feeling fire burning the hand, in the same way it may easily get the better of the lesser passions, but not of the most violent and strongest, except after the disturbance of the blood and spirits has been appeased}. The most that the will can do while this disturbance is in full force is not to yield to its effects, and to restrain many of the motions to which it inclines the body. {For example, if anger causes us to lift our hand to strike, the will can usually hold it back; if fear excites our legs to flee, the will can stop them, and so on in other cases.} [39]All the conflict we are in the habit of conceiving to exist between the lower part of the soul we call sensitive, and the upper, rational one, or, as we may say, between the natural appetites and the will, consists only in the opposition between the motions that the body, through its spirits, and the soul, through its will, tend to excite at the same time in the gland. For there is within us but one soul, and this soul does not in itself have any diversity of parts; the same part which is sensitive is rational, and all the soul's appetites are volitions. {The error committed in making the soul play the part of various personages, usually in opposition to one another, proceeds only from the fact that we have not properly distinguished its functions from those of the body, to which alone we must attribute everything observable in us that is opposed to our reason. Thus, there is no conflict here, except that the small gland existing in the middle of the brain, being capable of being thrust to one side by the soul, and to the other by the animal spirits—which, as I said earlier, are mere bodies—it often happens that these two impulses are contrary, and that the stronger one obstructs the effect of the other.} However, we may distinguish two kinds of motions excited in the gland by the spirits. The ones represent to the soul the objects moving the senses, or the impressions encountered in the brain, and make no attempt to affect its will. The others make an effort to do so—that is, the efforts that cause the passions or the motions of the body accompanying the passions. {And as

---

39. Art. 47. *In what the conflict we imagine existing between the lower and higher part of the soul consists.*

to the former, although they often hinder the actions of the soul, or else are hindered by them, yet, because they are not directly contrary to them, we do not notice any conflict between them. We notice only the conflict between the latter and the acts of will that conflict with them, as for example, between the effort by which the spirits push the gland to cause in the soul a desire for something, and the one with which the soul repels it by the will it has to avoid the very same thing. And what chiefly causes this conflict to appear is that the will, not having the power to excite the passions directly, as has already been said, is constrained to use its industry, and to apply itself to consider successively several things as to which, although it happens that one has the power to change for a moment the course taken by the spirits, it may turn out that what follows does not have this power, and that the spirits may immediately afterward revert to that same course because the previous arrangement in the nerves, heart, and blood has not changed, and thus it comes about that the soul feels itself almost at the same time impelled to desire and not to desire the same thing. It is this that has occasioned our imagining in the soul two powers in conflict with one another.} At the same time, we may still conceive a sort of conflict, inasmuch as the same cause exciting some passion in the soul often also excites certain motions in the body to which the soul does not contribute, and which it stops, or tries to stop, as soon as it perceives them—as we see when what excites fear also causes the spirits to enter into the muscles serving to move the legs with the object of flight, and when the will we have to be brave stops them from doing so. [40]Now it is from the success of these conflicts that each person can discover the strength or weakness of his soul. For those in whom the will can naturally conquer the passions most easily, and stop the motions of the body accompanying them, without doubt possess the strongest souls. But there are some who cannot feel their strength because they never cause their will to do battle with its proper weapons, but only with weapons provided to it by some passions so that it can resist some others. What I call the will's proper arms are firm and determinate judgments concerning the knowledge of good and evil, according to which it has resolved to conduct the actions of its life. {And the weakest souls of all are those whose will does not thus determine itself to follow certain judgments but allows

---

40. Art. 48. *How we recognize the strength or weakness of souls, and what is lacking in the weakest souls.*

itself continually to be carried away by its present passions, which, being frequently contrary to one another, draw the will first to one side, then to the other, and, by pulling it into conflict with itself, place the soul in the most deplorable condition. Thus, when fear represents death as an extreme evil that can be avoided only by flight, and if ambition presents the infamy of this flight as an evil worse than death, these two passions agitate the will in different ways, which, obeying one and then the other, is in continual opposition to itself, and thus enslaves the soul and renders it unhappy.} [41]And it is useful here to know that, as was already said above, although from the beginning of our life each motion of the gland seems to have been joined by nature to each one of our thoughts, we may at the same time join them to others by habit. [. . .] They can at the same time be separated from these by habit and joined to others that are very different; moreover, this habit can be acquired through a single action, and does not require long usage. Thus, when we unexpectedly meet with something very bad in food that we are eating with relish, the surprise this event gives us may so change the disposition of our brain that we can no longer see any such food without revulsion.

The Specific Passions[42]

[43]It is known {from what was said above} that the ultimate and most proximate cause of the passions of the soul is nothing but the agitation with which the spirits move the little gland in the middle of the brain. {But this is not sufficient to distinguish them from one another; we must seek their origins and examine their first causes. Now, they can sometimes be caused by the action of the soul, which sets itself to conceive this or that object, and by the mere temperament of the body or by the impressions accidentally found in the brain, as it happens when one feels sad or joyful without being able to say on what account. From what has been said,} it appears, however, that all the same passions can also be excited

---

41. Art. 49. *The strength of the soul is not sufficient without the knowledge of the truth* is omitted. From Art. 50. *There is no soul so feeble that it cannot, if well directed, acquire an absolute power over its passions.*
42. From AT XI, 371–442. Original title: The Number and Order of the Passions and the Explanation of the Six Primitive Passions.
43. Art. 51. *The primary causes of passions.*

by the objects moving the senses, and that these objects are their more common and principal causes. {From this it follows that, to find them all, it suffices to consider all the effects of these objects.} [44]I observe, in addition, that the objects moving the senses do not excite various passions in us because of the differences in them, but only because of the various ways that they can harm or benefit us, or in general be important to us. The function of all the passions consists in this alone, that they dispose the soul to want the things nature deems useful to us, and to persist in this volition; and the same agitation of the spirits that normally causes the passions also disposes the body to the motions serving to perform these things.[45] [46]I know very well that[47] <others> derive their enumeration of the passions from the distinction they draw, in the sensitive part of the soul, between two appetites, one they call "concupiscible" and the other "irascible." And because I do not recognize any distinction of parts in the soul {as I said above,} this seems to mean nothing else to me except that it has two faculties, one of desire and the other of anger; and since the soul has in the same way the faculties of wonder, love, hope, and fear, {and thus to receive in itself each of the other passions, or to perform the actions to which these passions impel it,} I do not see why these others wanted to refer them all to desire or anger.[48] [49]{But the number of simple

---

44. Art. 52. *The function of the passions and how they can be enumerated.*

45. Omitted: Hence, to enumerate them, we only need to examine, in order, in how many ways mattering to us our senses can be moved by their objects. And here I will enumerate all the principal passions in the order in which they can be found. Section title between Art. 52 and 53: The Order and Number of the Passions. Omitted are Art. 53. *Wonder*; 54. *Esteem and contempt, generosity or pride,* and *humility or abjectness*; 55. *Reverence and disdain*; 56. *Love and hatred*; 57. *Desire*; 58. *Hope, fear, jealousy, confidence, and despair*; 59. *Irresolution, courage, boldness, emulation, cowardice, and terror*; 60. *Remorse*; 61. *Joy and sadness*; 62. *Derision, envy, pity*; 63. *Self-satisfaction and repentance*; 64. *Favor and gratitude*; 65. *Indignation and anger*; 66. *Pride and shame*; and 67. *Disgust, regret, and cheerfulness*.

46. Art. 68. *Why this enumeration of the passions is different from the commonly accepted one.* Omitted: This order seems to me best for enumerating the passions.

47. Omitted: I deviate from the opinion of all those who wrote about this before, but not without good reason. For they

48. Omitted: Apart from their enumeration not including all the principal passions, as I think this one does, I am speaking only of the principal passions, because one could still distinguish several more specific ones, and their number is indefinite.

49. Art. 69. *There are only six primitive passions.*

and primitive passions is not very large. For, in reviewing all those that I enumerated, one can easily observe that} there are only six *primitive* passions, namely: *wonder, love, hatred, desire, joy*, and *sadness*. {All the others are composed from some of these six or are species of them. Therefore, in order that their multitude not inconvenience the readers, I will treat the six primitive passions here separately.} <The number of the other passions is indefinite,>[50] but later I will show how all the others originate from the primitive passions.

Wonder

<The first of the primitive passions is> [51]*wonder*. It is a sudden surprise of the soul, causing the soul to consider attentively objects that seem rare and extraordinary to it. [52]And this passion is {unique in that we find that} it is not accompanied by any change in the heart and in the blood, as are the other passions. {The reason for this is that,} having neither good nor evil for its object, but only the knowledge of the thing we wonder at {it has no relation to the heart and blood, on which depends all the well-being of the body}. The change only happens in relation to the brain {where the sense organs serving to provide this knowledge are located}. [53]{This does not prevent it from having a lot of strength on account of the surprise, that is, the sudden and unexpected arrival of the impression which changes the motion of the spirits. Such surprise is proper and specific to this passion, so that when it occurs in other passions (and it normally occurs in and increases almost all of them), it is because wonder is joined with them.} And its strength depends on two things, namely, its novelty and the motion it causes being at full strength from its beginning. {For it is certain that such a motion has more effect than one which, being weak initially and increasing only gradually, can easily be diverted.} This is because the

---

50. From Art. 68.
51. Art. 70. *Wonder, its definition and its cause*. Omitted: So it is caused first by an impression in the brain that represents the object as rare and consequently worthy of serious consideration; and second by a motion of the spirits, which the impression disposes to tend with great force toward the place of the brain where it is located, so as to strengthen and preserve it; and also to pass from there into the muscles serving to retain the sense organs in the same situation in which they are, so that if it was formed by them it may still be maintained by them.
52. Art. 71. *There occurs no change in the heart or in the blood in this passion*.
53. Art. 72. *What the strength of wonder consists of*.

novel objects of the senses touch the brain in certain parts where it is not normally touched; and since these parts are softer or less firm than those hardened by frequent agitation, the effect of the motions they excite there is increased. {We will not think this incredible if we consider that for similar reasons the soles of our feet, accustomed to a rather harsh contact by the weight of the body they bear, allow us to only feel very little of that contact when we walk; instead, we find a much smaller and softer contact that tickles them almost unbearably just because it is not ordinary to us.} [54]*Astonishment* is an excess of wonder that can never be anything but bad. [55]And wonder, in particular, can be said to be helpful in making us learn and retain in our memory things of which we were previously unaware. For we only wonder at what seems rare and extraordinary to us {and something can appear so to us only because we were unaware of it, or perhaps because it is different from the things we have known, for this difference makes us call it extraordinary. Now, when something that was unknown to us presents itself again to our understanding or to our senses, this does not occasion us to retain it in our memory, unless the idea we have of it is strengthened by our brain by some passion, or even by the application of our understanding, which our will determines to a particular attention and reflection. The other passions can serve to make people observe things that look good or bad, but we only have wonder for those that merely seem rare}. Thus, we see that those who have no natural inclination to this passion are usually very ignorant. [56]{Moreover, although only those who are dull and stupid are not naturally disposed to wonder,} this is not to say that those who have the best minds are always the most inclined to it, but mainly that those who, although they have a rather good common sense, nevertheless do not have a high opinion of their sufficiency. [57]But there is no other remedy for excessive wonder than to acquire the knowledge of many things, and to practice contemplation of all the ones that may seem the most rare and strange. [58]Its excess can become a habit when we neglect

---

54. From Art. 73. *What astonishment is.* Art. 74. *How the passions are useful and how they are harmful* is omitted.

55. Art. 75. *How wonder is particularly useful.*

56. Art. 77. *It is not the most stupid or clever people who are most captivated by wonder.*

57. From Art. 76. *In what way it can be harmful, and how we can make up for its deficiency and correct its excess.*

58. Title of Art 78. *Its excess can become a habit when we neglect to correct it.* The rest is omitted except for the last sentence of the article.

to correct it. For those who are *blindly curious* gradually become such that things of no importance are no less capable of detaining them than ones whose inquiry is more useful.

Love and Hatred

⁵⁹*Love* is an emotion of the soul caused by the motion of spirits, which incite the soul to join willingly to objects that appear to be suitable for it. And *hatred* is an emotion caused by the spirits, which incite the soul to want to be separated from the objects presenting themselves to it as harmful. {I say that these emotions are caused by the spirits, as much to distinguish love and hatred, which are passions and depend on the body, from the judgments that also cause the soul to join itself willingly to the things it considers good and separate itself from those it considers bad, as to distinguish them from the emotions these judgments alone excite in the soul.} ⁶⁰Moreover, by the term willingly, I do not intend to speak of desire here, which is a separate passion and relates to the future, but of the consent by which we now consider ourselves as joined with what we love, such that we imagine a whole, of which we think we are only a part and the thing loved is another such part. On the other hand, in hatred we consider ourselves alone as a whole entirely separated from the thing for which we have some aversion. ⁶¹<We distinguish two kinds of love, *benevolent* and *concupiscent*.>⁶² But it seems to me that this distinction concerns only the effects of love, and not its essence. {For as soon as we have willingly joined ourselves to some object, of whatever nature, we feel benevolence toward it, that is, we also willingly join to it the things we believe to be suitable for it; this is one of the principal effects of love. And if we judge that it would be good to possess or be associated with it other than willingly, we desire it; this is also one of the most ordinary effects of love.} ⁶³We can, I think, more reasonably distinguish love through the esteem we have

387

388

389
390

---

59. Art. 79. *The definitions of love and hatred.*
60. Art. 80. *What it is for the soul to join or separate itself willingly.*
61. Art. 81. *On the distinction we commonly make between concupiscent and benevolent love.*
62. Original text: Now, we commonly distinguish two kinds of love, one of which is called benevolent love, which prompts us to want the well-being of what we love; the other is called concupiscent love, which makes us desire the thing we love.
63. Art. 82. *How very different passions concur in that they participate in love* is omitted. Art. 83. *The difference between simple affection, friendship, and devotion.*

for what we love, as compared with ourselves. For when we esteem the object of our love as less than ourselves, we only have a simple affection for it <or *benevolence*>; when we esteem it as equal, it is called *friendship*; and when we esteem it more, the passion we have can be called *devotion*. [. . .] [64]Moreover, although hatred is directly opposed to love, we do not, however, distinguish it into as many species, because we do not observe as much difference between the evils from which we are separated willingly as we do between the goods to which we are joined. [65]I find only one significant distinction which is similar in love and hatred. {It consists in that the objects of both love and hatred can be represented to the soul by the external senses, or else by the internal ones and by its own reason. For we commonly call good or bad what our internal senses or our reason make us judge suitable or contrary to our nature; but we call beautiful or ugly what is represented as such to us by our external senses, mainly by that of sight, which we consider more than all the others.} From this arise two kinds of hatred, one relating to *bad* things, the other to *ugly* ones; the former can be called *horror* and the latter *repulsion*. This is opposed to *attraction*, the love we have for good and beautiful things.[66] But what is most remarkable here is that these passions of attraction and repulsion tend to be more violent than other kinds of love or hatred because what enters the soul through the senses touches it more strongly than what is represented to it by its reason. At the same time, however, they usually contain less truth. Thus, of all the passions, these are the most deceptive, and from which we must guard ourselves most carefully. [67]But when this knowledge of love is true, that is, when the things it brings us to love are truly good, and those it brings us to hate are truly bad, love is incomparably better than hatred. It cannot be too great, and it never fails to produce joy. [68]Hatred, on the other hand, cannot be so mild that it does not harm; and it is never without sadness. I say it cannot be too mild, because we cannot be incited to any action by the hatred of an evil more than we can be moved to it even

---

64. Art. 84. *There are not so many kinds of hatred as there are of love.*
65. Art. 85. *Attraction and repulsion.*
66. Sentence out of order. Original text: From this arise two kinds of love, namely, the love we have for good things and the love we have for beautiful things; we can give the name of attraction to the former, in order not to confuse it with the latter, or with desire, to which we often assign the name love.
67. From Art. 139. *The function of the same passions as they belong to the soul, and first of love.*
68. From Art. 140. *Hatred.*

better by the love of a contrary good, at least when the good and evil are sufficiently well known.

Desire

[69]The passion of *desire* is an agitation of the soul caused by spirits, which disposes the soul to want for the *future* the things it imagines to be suitable. {Thus, we desire not only the presence of goods that are absent, but also the preservation of goods that are present and the absence of evils, both those already affecting us and those we believe could befall us in the time to come.} [70]In the Schools they teach that desire is a passion with no contrary and commonly oppose the passion leading to the search for good[71] to the one leading to the avoidance of evil, which we call *aversion*. But {there is no good whose deprivation is not an evil and no evil considered as a positive thing whose deprivation is not a good. In seeking wealth, for example, we necessarily avoid poverty, while in avoiding illness we seek health, and so forth for the others. Thus,} I think it is always the same motion that leads to the search for good, and at the same time to the avoidance of evil, its contrary. {I observe only this difference, that the desire we have when we tend toward some good is accompanied by love, and then by hope and joy, whereas the same desire, when we tend to avoid the evil contrary to that good, is accompanied by hatred, fear, and sadness; this causes us to judge it as contrary to ourselves. But if we want to consider the desire when it also relates at the same time both to the pursuit of some good and to the avoidance of the opposite evil, we can see very clearly that} it is only *one* passion that constitutes both. [72]And I think the most common mistake we make about desires is that we do not distinguish enough between the things depending entirely on us from those that do not. As for the things depending on us alone, that is, on our free will, it suffices to know they are good to be unable to desire them too ardently. [73]As for the things not depending on us in any way, however good they may be, we should never desire them with passion, not only because they

---

69. Art. 86. *The definition of desire.*
70. Art. 87. *Desire is a passion that has no contrary.*
71. Original text: I know very well that commonly in the Schools they oppose the passion that leads to the search for good, which alone we call desire.
72. From Art. 144. *Desires whose occasion depends only on us.*
73. From Art. 145. *Desires depending only on other causes, and what fortune is.*

may not happen {and thereby distressing us still more that we wished for them more,} but mainly because by occupying our thoughts they distract us from caring about other things whose acquisition depends on us. There are two general remedies for these vain desires: the first is generosity {of which I will speak later}; the second is that we must frequently reflect on Divine Providence,[74] and <altogether banish> fortune as a chimera (arising only from an error of our understanding). [75]But because most of our desires extend to things not depending wholly on us or wholly on others, we must distinguish precisely what in them depends only on us, in order to extend our desire to that alone; moreover, although we must consider the outcome as entirely fatal and immutable, so that our desire does not concern itself with it, we must not fail to consider the reasons that provide more or less hope, so as to use them in regulating our actions. [76]{It would be more reasonable to distinguish desire into as many different kinds as there are different objects we seek. For example, curiosity, which is nothing more than a desire for knowledge, is very different from a desire for glory, and the latter from the desire for revenge, and so on for the others.} But it suffices here to know that there are as many species of desire as there are of love or hatred, and that the greatest and strongest are those arising from *attraction* and *repulsion*.

Joy

[77]*Joy* is a pleasant emotion of the soul consisting in the soul's enjoyment of some good that impressions in the brain represent to it as its own. {I say that the enjoyment of the good consists in this emotion, for in fact the soul receives no other benefit from all the goods it possesses; and as long as it receives no joy from them, we can say that it does not enjoy them any more than it would if it did not possess them. I add that the good is what the impressions of the brain represent to it as its own} so that we do not confuse this joy, which is a *passion*, with the purely *intellectual* joy arising in the soul solely through an action of the soul; we can say that

---

74. Omitted: and represent to ourselves that it is impossible for anything to happen otherwise than it has been determined from all eternity by that Providence; it is like a fatality or an immutable necessity we must set against fortune, to destroy it.

75. From Art. 146. *Those desires depending on us and others.*

76. Art. 88. *The various species of desire.*

77. Art. 91. *The definition of joy.*

it is a pleasant emotion the soul excites in and by itself, consisting in the enjoyment it has of the good which its understanding represents to it as its own. It is true that while the soul is joined to the body, this intellectual joy can hardly fail to be accompanied by the joy which is a passion. {For, as soon as our understanding perceives that we possess some good, although this good may be so different from everything that belongs to the body as to be completely unimaginable, the imagination cannot fail to form an immediate impression in the brain, from which follows the motion of the spirits that excites the passion of joy.} [78]Moreover, since hatred and sadness must be rejected by the soul, even when they proceed from true knowledge, they must be even more so when they arise from some false opinion. But it can be doubted whether love and joy are good when they rest on bad foundations; and it seems to me that if we consider them precisely as they are in themselves with respect to the soul, we can say that, although joy is less solid and love less beneficial than when they have a better foundation, they do not cease to be preferable to ill-founded sadness and hatred. {Thus, in the affairs of life where we cannot avoid the risk of being mistaken, we always do much better by inclining toward the passions that tend to good than toward those that regard evil, even though we only do so to avoid it.} And often even a false joy is better than a sadness whose cause is true. But I dare not say the same of love in relation to hatred. {For when hatred is just, it merely takes us away from a subject containing an evil from which it is good to be separated, whereas an unjust love joins us to things that can be harmful, or at least that do not deserve to be considered by us to the extent we do, which demeans and debases us.} [79]<But, to the extent it is referred to desire,> joy is usually more harmful than sadness, when they rest on equally bad foundations, because the latter, engendering restraint and fear, in some way disposes us to prudence, whereas the former makes those who abandon themselves to it inconsiderate and reckless.

Sadness

[80]Sadness is an unpleasant listlessness which consists in the discomfort the soul receives from some evil or the defect that the impressions in the brain represent to it as its own. There is also an *intellectual* sadness, which is not

---

78. Art. 142. *Joy and love, compared with sadness and hatred.*
79. From Art. 143. *The same passions, as they relate to desire.*
80. Art. 92. *The definition of sadness.*

passion, but which rarely fails to be accompanied by it. [81]{When intellectual joy or sadness thus excites the passion, its cause is sufficiently clear.} For we see from their definitions that joy results from our opinion that we possess some good, and sadness from our opinion that we possess some evil or defect. But it often happens that we feel sad or joyful without being able to observe distinctly the good or evil that are its causes, namely, when this good or evil forms its impressions in the brain without the intervention of the soul, {sometimes because they belong to the body alone, and sometimes also, although they belong to the soul, because it does not consider them as good or evil, but under some other form whose impression is joined in the brain to that good or evil}. [82]Thus, when we are in good health and things are calmer than usual, we feel in ourselves a cheerfulness that does not arise from any function of the understanding, but only from the impressions the motion of spirits forms in the brain; and we feel sad in the same way when our body is indisposed, although we do not know that it is. Thus, the tickling of the senses is followed so closely by joy, and pain by sadness, that most people do not distinguish between them. However, they differ so greatly that we can sometime experience pains with joy and receive tickles we find unpleasant. But what usually causes joy to follow tickling is that everything called tickling or pleasurable sensation consists in the objects of the senses exciting some motion in the nerves. [. . .] <But if the cause is violent, it may injure the nerves and produce pain and sadness.>[83]

[84]<The cause of the five preceding passions,>[85] unlike that of wonder, is not in the brain alone, but also in the heart, the spleen, the liver and in

---

81. Art. 93. *The causes of these two passions.*

82. Art. 94. *How these passions are excited by goods and evils which concern only the body and what tickle and pain consist of.*

83. Original text: And pain usually produces sadness because the sensation called pain always arises from some action so violent as to injure the nerves; this sensation, instituted by nature to signify to the soul the damage the body receives by this action, and the body's weakness in that it could not resist it, represents both as evils always disagreeable to it, except when they cause some good which it esteems more highly. Art. 95. *How they can also be excited by goods and evils which the soul does not notice, although they belong to it, such as are the pleasure we derive in taking risks or remembering past evil* is omitted.

84. From Art. 96. *The motions of the blood and the spirits that cause the five preceding passions.*

85. Original text: The five passions I began to explain here are so joined or opposed to one another that it is easier to consider them all together than to treat each one separately, as wonder was treated.

all other parts of the body, as they serve to produce the blood and then the spirits. <Indeed, power and efficacy, now milder, now more violent, differentiates among passions.> [86]And I deduce the reasons for all this from what I said above, that there is such a connection between our soul and our body that when we have once joined some bodily action with a thought, the one does not present itself afterward without the other also presenting itself.[87] [88]<If we examine the external signs of these passions, we see that> The main ones are *actions* of the eyes and face, *changes* in color <blushing or turning pale>, *trembling, listlessness, fainting* <or loss of consciousness>, *laughter*[89] (which, if it is explosive, always provides some slight occasion for hatred, or at least for wonder.[90] And those with unhealthy spleen are apt to be not only sadder, but also, at times, to be more cheerful and more disposed to laugh than the others. [91]As for the laughter sometimes accompanying indignation, it is usually artificial and feigned. But when it is natural, it seems to result from the joy we feel when we see that we cannot be hurt by the evil at which we are indignant), [92]*tears* (which do not result from an *extreme* sadness, but only from a moderate one, accompanied or followed by some feeling of love or joy.[93] [94]However, there are children who turn pale instead of crying when they are angry. This can indicate an extraordinary judgment and courage in them, {namely, when it results from their considering the magnitude of the evil and preparing

---

86. From Art. 107. *The cause of these motions in love.*
87. Omitted are Art. 108. *In hatred*; Art. 109. *In joy*; Art. 110. *In sadness*; and Art. 111. *In desire.*
88. From Art. 112. *The external signs of these passions.*
89. From Art. 126. *The main causes of laughter.* Omitted are Art. 113. *Actions of the eyes and face*; 114. *Changes of color*; 115. *How joy makes you blush*; 116. *How sadness makes you pale*; 118. *Trembling*; 119. *Listlessness*; 120. *How it is caused by love and desire;* 121. *It can also be caused by other passions*; 122. *Fainting*; 123. *Why we do not faint out of sadness*; 124. *Laughter*; and 125. *Why laughter does not accompany the greatest joys.*
90. Original text: Experience also shows us that in all encounters that can produce the explosive laughter coming from the lungs, there is always some slight occasion for hatred, or at least for wonder.
91. From Art. 127. *The cause of laughter in indignation.*
92. From Art. 128. *The origin of tears.*
93. Omitted are Art. 129. *How the vapors are changed into water*; 130. *How what causes pain in the eye makes it weep*; 131. *How we weep from sadness*; and 133. *Why children and the elderly weep readily.*
94. Art. 134. *Why some children turn pale instead of crying.*

themselves for solid resistance, in the same way as those who are older}. But <with children> it is more usually a mark of a bad nature, namely, when it results from being inclined to hatred or fear),⁹⁵ ⁹⁶*groans* (whose cries are usually more acute than those accompanying laughter, although they are produced in almost the same way), *sighs*. <If, however, some of the usual color is lacking (as when gloomy blushing is observed in sadness) it is entirely attributable to other passions, mixing and joining with each other.>⁹⁷

The Passions Following from the Primitive Passions[98]

The Passions Following from Wonder

⁹⁹Having explained the six primitive passions, <the others following from them remain to be explained>.¹⁰⁰ The first two of the latter are *esteem* and *contempt*; for, even though these names usually signify only opinions {we have without passion concerning the value of a thing}, however, because these opinions often give rise to passions to which no specific names have been given, I think that the previous terms can be attributed to them. And *esteem*, insofar as it is a passion, is an inclination of the soul to represent to itself the value of the thing esteemed; {this inclination being caused by a particular motion of the spirits so directed in the brain that they strengthen the impressions used to this

---

95. Omitted: for these are passions that diminish the matter of which tears are formed. And we see, on the other hand, that children who cry very easily are inclined to love and pity.
96. From Art. 132. *The groans accompanying tears*.
97. Paraphrasing from Art. 117. *How we often blush when sad*. The rest of Book II is omitted: Art. 135. *Sighs*; 136. *Where the effects of the passions peculiar to some people come from*; 139. *The function of the five passions insofar as they belong to the soul, and first that of love*; 140. *Hatred*; 141. *Desire, joy, and sadness*; and 148. *The exercise of virtue is a supreme remedy against the passions*. A few sentences of Art. 147, 137, and 138 are inserted toward the end of part III.
98. From AT XI, 443–88. Original title: The Specific Passions.
99. Art. 149. *Esteem and contempt*.
100. Omitted: which are like the genera of which all the others are species, I will here briefly remark on what is particular in each of the others, retaining the same order in which I enumerated them above.

effect}. On the other hand, the passion of *contempt* is an inclination of the soul to consider the baseness or insignificance of what it has contempt for {and is caused by the motion of spirits that strengthen the idea of this insignificance}. [101]Thus, these two passions are merely species of wonder. {For when we do not wonder at the greatness or insignificance of an object, making neither more nor less of it than reason tells us we should, then our esteem or contempt of it is without passion.} And, although esteem is often excited in us by love, and contempt by hate, this is not universal; it results only from our being more or less inclined to consider the greatness or insignificance of an object, given that we have more or less affection for it. [102]Now, these two passions can generally be referred to all kinds of objects; but they are chiefly significant when we refer them to ourselves, that is, when it is our own merit that we esteem or have contempt for. The motion of the spirits that causes them is then so manifest that it changes even the appearance, gestures, gait, and generally all the actions of those who conceive a better or a worse opinion of themselves than is ordinary. [103]{And since one of the principal parts of wisdom is to know how and for what reason a person should esteem or have contempt for himself, I will try to express my opinion of this.} I observe in us only one thing that can give us just reason to esteem ourselves, namely the use of our free will, and the control we have over our volitions. {For we can rightly be praised or blamed only for the actions that depend upon this free will, and it renders us in a way like God by making us masters of ourselves, provided we do not allow ourselves to lose the rights it gives us through pusillanimity.} [104]Thus, I believe that true *generosity* (which causes a person's self-esteem to be as great as it legitimately can be) consists, in part, only in knowing that nothing really belongs to a person but this free disposition of his volitions and that he should be praised or blamed for no other reason than he uses them well or badly, and, in part, in his feeling in himself a firm and constant resolution to use it well, that is, never to lack the will to undertake and carry out whatever he judges to be best.

445

446

---

101. Art. 150. *These two passions are merely species of wonder.*
102. Art. 151. *We can esteem or have contempt for ourselves.*
103. Art. 152. *For what reason we can esteem ourselves.*
104. Art. 153. *What generosity consists of.*

This is to follow virtue perfectly. [105]'Those who possess this knowledge and feeling about themselves {easily convince themselves that any other person can have this same knowledge and feeling of themselves, because it involves nothing that depends on others. That is why they} never have contempt for anyone. {Although they often see that others commit misdeeds that show their weakness, they are nevertheless more inclined to excuse than to blame them, and to believe that} it is rather for lack of knowledge than for lack of good will that others commit them. And, as they do not consider themselves as much inferior to those who have more goods or honor, or even more intelligence, more knowledge, more beauty, or generally who surpass them in some other perfections, also they do not esteem themselves much above those whom they surpass. {For, all these things seem to them to be unimportant, compared to good will, for which they alone esteem themselves, and which they also suppose to be present, or at least capable of being present, in every other person.} [106]'Those generous in this way are naturally inclined to do great deeds, and at the same time not to undertake anything they do not feel themselves capable of doing. And because they esteem nothing greater than doing good to others and having contempt for their self-interest, they are always perfectly courteous, affable, and accommodating to everyone. {And thus, they are entirely masters over their passions, especially desire, jealousy, and envy, because there is nothing else whose acquisition depends on them which they think is sufficiently valuable to be worth pursuing; similarly with hatred toward other people, because they esteem everyone; and fear, because the confidence they have in their virtue gives them self-assurance; and finally anger, because valuing little everything that depends on others, they never give their enemies so much advantage as to admit that they are hurt by them.} [107]'Thus, the most generous people are usually the humblest; and *humility* as a virtue consists only in the reflection we make on the infirmity of our nature {and on misdeeds we may previously have committed or can commit, which are no less serious than those others may commit}. It is why we do not prefer ourselves to anyone {and think that others having their

---

105. Art. 154. *How generosity prevents us from being contemptuous of others.*
106. Art. 156. *The properties of generosity and how generosity serves as a remedy against all the disturbances of the passions.*
107. Art. 155. *What humility as a virtue consists in.*

free will as much as we do, can use it as well as we do}. [108]As for abjectness or humility as a vice, it consists mainly in feeling weak or unresolved, and in not being able to refrain from doing things we know we will regret afterward, as if we lacked the full use of our free will. It also involves the belief that we cannot subsist by ourselves or do without things whose acquisition depends upon others. Thus, it is directly opposed to generosity. Generous people are no more elated by prosperity than humbled by adversity,[109] such that those with abject minds are the most arrogant and pretentious {just as the most generous are the most modest and most humble. But, whereas those with a strong and generous spirit do not change their mood to suit the prosperities or adversities that befall upon them, those with a weak and abject spirit are guided only by fortune}. We even often see the latter abase themselves shamefully before those from whom they expect some advantage or fear some evil, and at the same time they raise themselves impudently above those from whom they hope or fear nothing. [110]*Vanity*[111] is always a great vice, and it is even more so as the reason such people esteem themselves is more groundless. The most groundless reason is when people are vain without cause, that is, without thinking that there is any merit in them for which they should be valued, but only because they do not make much of merit, imagining glory to be nothing but an appropriation, thus believing that those who claim the most merit for themselves possess the most merit. {This vice is so unreasonable and absurd, that I would find it hard to believe that people would indulge in it, if no one was ever praised without grounds. But flattery is so common everywhere that there is no person whose faults are so great that he does not often see himself esteemed for things that are not praiseworthy, or even that are blameworthy.} <Its cause is most often flattery,> which gives opportunities for the most ignorant and stupid people to fall into this kind of vanity. [112]Moreover, it is easy to understand that vanity and abjectness are not only vices, but also passions, because their emotion

---

108. Art. 159. *Humility as a vice.*

109. Sentence out of order.

110. Art. 157. *Vanity.*

111. Omitted: All those who conceive a good opinion of themselves for some other cause, whatever it may be, do not possess real generosity, but only a vanity.

112. Art. 158. *The effects of vanity are contrary to those of generosity* is omitted. From Art. 160. *The motion of the spirits in these passions.*

is very evident on the external features of those who are suddenly uplifted or downcast by some new occasion. But we can doubt whether generosity and humility, which are virtues, can also be passions, since their motions are less apparent; it seems that virtue does not play as great a role with passion as vice does. However, I do not see any reason preventing the same motion of spirits serving to strengthen a thought with a bad foundation, from also being able to strengthen it with a proper one. [113]We should note that what we commonly call virtues are habits in the soul which dispose it to certain thoughts. Thus, they are different from thoughts, but can produce them and be produced by them. We should also note that thoughts can be produced by the soul alone. But it often happens that some motion of the spirits strengthens them; as a result, they are actions of virtue and at the same time passions of the soul. [114]*Veneration* or *respect* is an inclination of the soul not only to esteem the object it reveres, but also to submit to it with some fear, to try to gain its favor. Thus, we have veneration only for the free causes we deem capable of doing us good or evil, without our knowing which they will do. For we have love and devotion rather than simple veneration for those from whom we expect only good, and we have hatred for those from whom we expect only evil; {and if we do not judge the cause of this good or this evil to be free, we do not submit to it to try to gain its favor. Thus, when the pagans had veneration for woods, springs, or mountains, it was not properly speaking these dead things they revered, but the deities that they believed presided over them}. And the motion of the spirits that excites this passion is composed of the one that excites wonder together with the one that excites awe (about which I will speak below). [115]What I call *disdain* is the inclination of the soul to despise a free cause by judging that, although by its nature it can do good and evil, it is nevertheless so far beneath us that it can do neither to us. And the motion of spirits that excites it is composed of those exciting wonder and confidence or boldness. [116]And it is generosity and weakness of mind or abjectness that determines the good or evil function of these two passions <that is, veneration and disdain>.

---

113. From Art. 161. *How generosity can be acquired.*
114. Art. 162. *Veneration.*
115. Art. 163. *Disdain.*
116. From Art. 164. *The function of these two passions.*

Chapter II   41

The Passions Following from Love and Hatred

[117]*Favor* is properly a desire to see good happen to someone for whom we have good will; {but I am using the word here to signify this will insofar as it is excited in us by some good action by the person for whom we have it. For we are naturally inclined to love those who do what we esteem as good, even though we receive no benefit from it}. Favor {in this sense} is a species of *love*, not of desire, although the desire to see good happen to the person favored always accompanies it. {And it is usually joined to pity because the misfortunes we see happening to unfortunate people cause us to reflect more on their merits.} [118]Gratitude is also a kind of love excited in us by some action of the person for whom we have it, because we believe that the person did us some good, or at least that he had this intention. [119]As for ingratitude, {it is not a passion, for nature did not put in us any motion of the spirits arousing it}. It is simply a vice directly opposed to gratitude insofar as gratitude is always virtuous and is one of the main bonds of human society. Consequently, this vice belongs only to brutish and foolish, arrogant people who think that all things are their due, or to stupid ones who do not reflect on the benefits they receive, or to weak and abject ones who, feeling their infirmity and need, basely seek the help of others, and hate them after receiving it; lacking the will to reciprocate, or despairing of their ability to do so, thinking that everyone is greedy like them and that no good is ever done without the hope of recompense, they think they deceived their benefactors. [120]*Indignation* is a species of hatred or aversion which we naturally have toward those who do any evil, of whatever nature. It is often mixed in with envy or pity; however, it has an entirely different object. For we are indignant only toward those who do good, or evil, to people who do not deserve it, but envy those who receive such a good, and pity those who receive the evil. {It is true that to possess a good we do not deserve is in some way to do evil. This may be the reason why Aristotle and his followers, assuming envy always to be a vice, called by

---

117. Art. 192. *Favor.*
118. From Art. 193. *Gratitude.*
119. Art. 194. *Ingratitude.*
120. Art. 195. *Indignation.*

the name indignation the envy which is not a vice.} [121]Indignation is also often accompanied by wonder. {For we are accustomed to assuming that everything will be done the way we think it should be done, that is, the way we think it good.} That is why, when it happens otherwise, it surprises us, and we wonder at it. Indignation is also not incompatible with joy, even though it is more commonly joined to sadness. {For when an evil about which we are indignant cannot harm us, and we consider that we would not want to do such a thing, it gives us some pleasure; and this is perhaps one of the causes of the laughter that sometimes accompanies this passion.} [122]Indignation is observed more in those who want to appear virtuous than in those who really are. [123]*Anger* is also a species of hatred {or of aversion} that we have toward those who have done some harm, or who tried to do harm, not just to anyone, but especially to us. [124]Those who are caused to become flush in anger are less to be feared than those it causes to turn pale. {And the external signs of this passion differ, according to the various temperaments of people and the diversity of the other passions composing or joined to it. Thus, we see some turning pale or trembling when they get angry, and others become flushed or even weep; it is usually thought that the anger of those who turn pale is more to be feared than is the anger of those who become flushed.} This is because, when explaining ourselves through our expressions and words, we expend all our heat in becoming flush;[125] <in pallor,> on the other hand, those who restrain themselves and resolve to greater vengeance become sad at the thought they are obligated to do so by the action making them angry. And they also sometimes fear the evils that may ensue from the resolution they took; this at first turns them pale, cold, and trembling. But later, when they come to take their

---

121. Art. 196. *Why indignation is sometimes joined to pity, and sometimes to derision* is omitted. Art. 197. *Indignation is often accompanied by wonder and is not incompatible with joy.*
122. From Art. 198. *The function of indignation.*
123. From Art. 199. *Anger.*
124. Art. 200. *Why those who are caused to become flush in anger are less to be feared than those it causes to turn pale.* The sentence is taken from the title of the article.
125. Original text: The reason for which is that when we are unwilling or unable to take revenge other than through our expressions and words, we expend all our heat and energy from the start when we are moved, which causes us to turn red; moreover, sometimes we cannot take revenge in any other way, we have such regret and self-pity that we are caused to weep.

revenge, they become warm again in greater degree from their initial coldness, just as we see that the fevers starting with a chill are usually the strongest. [126]This informs us that we can distinguish *two* kinds of anger: a very quick one manifesting itself powerfully on the outside but having little effect and being easily appeased; and another one that may not be so apparent at first but gnaws more at the heart and has more dangerous effects. Those with a lot of kindness and love are more prone to the first. For it does not result from a deep hatred, but from a sudden aversion surprising them, because they are inclined to imagine that all things should happen in the way they judge best, and so they wonder at and take offense as soon as things turn out otherwise, often even without the thing affecting them specifically. [. . .] [127]<Generosity serves as a remedy against the excesses of the most pernicious anger.>

The Passions Following from Desire, Joy, and Sadness

[128]*Hope* is a disposition of the soul to persuade itself that what it desires will come to pass. It is caused by a particular motion of the spirits, namely, the motion of *joy* mixed with that of desire. *Fear* is another disposition of the soul to persuade itself that what it desires will not come about *eventually*. It should be noted that although these two passions are contrary, we can nevertheless have them both together, namely, when we represent to ourselves various reasons at the same time, of which some have us regard the fulfilment of our desire as easy, and others make it seem difficult. [129]*Confidence* occurs when hope is so strong that it completely chases fear away. {Hope then changes its nature and is called confidence or assurance. And, when we are assured that what we desire will come to pass, even though we continue to want it to do so, we nevertheless cease to be agitated by the passion of desire, which made us seek the outcome anxiously.} *Despair* occurs when the fear is so extreme that it takes away all hope; despair, representing the thing desired as impossible, entirely

---

126. Art. 201. *There are two kinds of anger, and those who are most kind are most prone to the first*; Art. 202. *The weak and abject souls let themselves be carried away most by the second* is omitted.

127. From the title of Art. 203. *Generosity serves as a remedy against the excesses of anger.*

128. Art. 165. *Hope and fear.*

129. Art. 166. *Confidence and despair.* Omitted: Neither of these passions ever accompany desire without leaving some room for the other.

extinguishes hope, since hope only bears on possible things. [130]*Jealousy* is a species of fear related to our desire to retain possession of some good. It does not result as much from the strength of the reasons making us believe that the good can be lost, as from the high esteem we have of it. It causes us to examine even the slightest grounds as subjects for suspicion, and to take them as very considerable reasons. [131]This passion can be honest when we are careful to conserve the goods that are not the lesser ones. [132]<It is blameworthy when we are overly careful and only relate to others with suspicion and distrust.> [133]*Irresolution* is also a species of fear; that is why it is not a passion, unless our fear of choosing badly increases our uncertainty.[134] Keeping the soul in balance between several actions it can perform, irresolution causes it not to perform any of them, and thus gives the soul time to choose before determining itself. In this respect it truly has a beneficial function. But when irresolution lasts longer than necessary, and we spend in deliberation the time required for us to act, it is very bad. Now, I say it is a species of fear, even though it can happen that, when we have the choice of several things whose goodness seem equal, we remain uncertain and unresolved without any fear. [135]*Courage*, when it is a passion and not a habit {or natural inclination}, is a certain heat or agitation disposing the soul to apply itself vigorously to carry out what it wants to do, whatever its nature. And *boldness* is a species of courage disposing the soul to carry out the most dangerous ones. [136]Moreover, *emulation* is also a species of courage, but in another sense. For we can consider courage as a genus divided into as many species as it has different objects, and into as many others as it has causes. Boldness is a species of courage in the first sense, emulation in the second. The latter is nothing but a heat disposing the soul to undertake things it hopes it can achieve because it sees others succeed in them. Thus, it is a species of courage of which the external cause is an example. [137]*Pusillanimity* is directly opposed to courage. It

---

130. Art. 167. *Jealousy*.
131. From Art. 168. *In what way jealousy can be honest*.
132. From Art. 169. *In what way jealousy can be blameworthy*.
133. From Art. 170. *Irresolution*.
134. Sentence out of order.
135. Art. 171. *Courage and boldness*.
136. From Art. 172. *Emulation*.
137. Art. 173. *How boldness depends on hope* is omitted; Art. 174. *Pusillanimity and fear*.

is a languor or coldness preventing the soul from carrying out the things it would perform if it were free from this passion. And *fear* {or terror}, which is contrary to boldness, is not only a coldness, but also a turmoil and astonishment of the soul, which deprives it of the power to resist the evils it thinks are nearby. [138]Although I cannot persuade myself that nature has given us a passion which is always vicious and has no good and praiseworthy function, I still have a hard time determining what purpose these two passions can serve. [139]*Remorse* of conscience is a species of sadness resulting from our doubting whether something we are doing or have done is good or not; and it necessarily presupposes doubt. [140]*Derision* {or ridicule} is a species of joy mixed with hatred, resulting from our perceiving some slight evil in a person we think deserves it. We have hatred of this evil and are joyful to see it in someone who deserves it. [141]The most imperfect people are usually the most derisive. For, desiring to see all the others as misfortunate as they are, they are quite pleased with the evils that befall them, which they think they deserve. [142]As for moderate *mockery*, which usefully accentuates vices by making them appear ridiculous, without however our laughing at them or showing any hatred toward people, it is not a passion, but a quality of an honorable person. It brings out the cheerfulness of his temper and the tranquility of his soul. {These are signs of virtue and often also the dexterity of his mind, in that the person knows how to give a pleasant aspect to what he laughs at.} [143]And it is not dishonorable to laugh when we hear another's mockery; it may even be sorrowful not to laugh. But when we engage in mockery ourselves, it is more proper not to laugh, so as not to seem surprised by the things we say or wonder at our skill in making them up. And this makes them even more surprising to those who hear them. [144]*Envy*, insofar as it is a passion, is a species of sadness mixed in with hatred, resulting from seeing some good come to those we think undeserving of it. This is something that can only rightly be thought of with respect to goods due

---

138. From Art. 175. *The function of pusillanimity.*
139. Art. 176. *The function of fear* is omitted. From Art. 177. *Remorse.*
140. From Art. 178. *Derision.*
141. From Art. 179. *Why the most imperfect people are usually the most derisive.*
142. Art. 180. *The function of mockery.*
143. Art. 181. *The function of laughter in mockery.*
144. From Art. 182. *Envy.*

to fortune. ¹⁴⁵If envy is excited in us only because we naturally love justice, and thus become upset that it is not observed in the distribution of these goods, as long as envy relates solely to the bad distribution of these goods, it can be excusable, but if it is directed against the people who possess or distribute them, <it is improper and inexcusable>. ¹⁴⁶Envious people usually have a leaden complexion, that is, pale, mixed with yellow and black, like blood in a bruise, [. . .] but we should not think that everyone in whom we see this color is inclined to envy. ¹⁴⁷*Pity* is a species of sadness mixed in with love or good will toward those whom we see suffering some evil we think they do not deserve. {Thus, it is contrary to envy because of its object, and to derision because the object is considered in a different way.} ¹⁴⁸Those who feel very weak and prone to the adversities of fortune seem more inclined to this passion than others. ¹⁴⁹<It differs from generosity, in that the sadness of the kind of pity caused by generosity> is not bitter; and, like the one caused by the tragic actions one sees represented in the theater, it is more external, more in the senses than in the interior of the soul. ¹⁵⁰But only evil and envious, brutish, and desperate minds are insensitive to pity.¹⁵¹ ¹⁵²The *self-satisfaction* <or *self-acceptance*> of those who steadfastly follow virtue is a habit of their souls called tranquility and ease of conscience. ¹⁵³*Repentance* is directly contrary to self-satisfaction and results from our believing we have performed an evil deed; and it is very bitter, because its cause lies in ourselves alone. ¹⁵⁴*Pride* is a species of joy based on our love for ourselves and resulting from our belief or hope of being praised by others. Thus, it is different from the internal satisfaction resulting from our believing we performed

---

145. From Art. 183. *How envy can be proper or improper.*
146. From Art. 184. *How it happens that envious people have a leaden complexion.*
147. Art. 185. *Pity.*
148. From Art. 186. *Those most given to pity.*
149. From Art. 187. *How the most generous are affected by this passion.*
150. Art. 188. *Those not affected by this passion.*
151. Original text: But only evil and envious minds, who naturally hate all people, or else those who are so brutish and so blinded by good fortune or made desperate by bad fortune that they do not think any more harm can befall them, are insensitive to pity. Art. 189. *Why this passion moves us to tears* is omitted.
152. From Art. 190. *Self-satisfaction.*
153. From Art. 191. *Repentance.*
154. From Art. 204. *Pride.*

a good action. ¹⁵⁵*Shame* {in contrast, is a species of sadness based also on self-love, and} results from our belief or fear of being blamed. It is, in addition, a species of modesty or humility and anxiety about ourselves. For, when our self-esteem is so strong that we cannot imagine anyone looking down on us, we cannot easily be ashamed. ¹⁵⁶Now, pride and shame have the same function in that they incite us to virtue, the one through hope, the other through fear. We only need to instruct our judgment concerning what is truly deserving of blame or praise, so as not to be ashamed of doing well, and not to take pride in our vices, as many do. But it is not good to let go of these passions entirely, as the *Cynics* used to do. For, although people judge very badly, however, because we cannot live without them and it is important for us to be valued by them, we must often follow their opinions rather than our own regarding the external appearance of our actions. ¹⁵⁷*Impudence* {or brazenness, which is a contempt for shame, and often also for pride} is not a passion, because there is no specific motion of spirits in us that excites it; rather, it is a vice opposite to shame as well as to pride {insofar as they are both good, just as ingratitude is opposed to gratitude and cruelty to pity}. And the main cause of brazenness results from our having received several great insults. {For when we are young, we imagine praise to be a good and infamy an evil of much greater importance in life than experience shows them to be.} When this happens, we see ourselves completely deprived of honor and despised by everyone. That is why people who assess good and evil only through the comforts of the body become brazen; they see that they enjoy these comforts after the insults as well as they did before, or sometimes even better, because they are free from the many constraints to which honor obliged them {and, if loss of property is attached to their disgrace, there are charitable persons who will make up their loss}. ¹⁵⁸*Distaste* <or disgust in French> is a species of sadness {resulting from the same cause as joy previously did}. For we are so constituted that most of the things we enjoy are good for us only for a while, and afterward become displeasing. This is apparent mainly with drinking and eating, which are valuable only when we have an appetite, and harmful when we no longer

---

155. Art. 205. *Shame*.
156. Art. 206. *The function of these two passions*.
157. From Art. 207. *Impudence*.
158. Art. 208. *Disgust*.

do. {And because they then cease to be pleasant to the taste, we call this passion disgust.} [159] *Regret* is also a species of sadness {which has a particular bitterness, in that it is always joined to some despair and to the memory of the pleasure that has given us the enjoyment. For we only regret the goods that we have enjoyed, and} that come from goods that are so lost that we have no hope of recovering them at the time and in the manner that we regret them. [160] {Finally, what I call} *cheerfulness* is a species of joy that is singular in that its sweetness is increased by the memory of the evils we have suffered and from which we feel unburdened, in the same way as when we feel ourselves relieved of some heavy burden we carried on our shoulders for a long time. I do not see anything very remarkable in these three passions; hence, I placed them here only to have <pointed them out>.[161] [162] <We cannot> receive any disadvantage from the passions; clearly, our good and our evil depend mainly on internal emotions agitated in the soul only by the soul itself. In this they differ from those passions, which always depend on some motion of the spirits. And although these emotions of the soul are often joined to passions which are similar to them, they can often be found with others as well, and even arise from some contrary to them. For example, when a husband mourns his dead wife[163] and nonetheless feels a secret joy in the innermost part of his soul, the emotion of this joy would have so much power that the accompanying sadness and tears would not be able to diminish its force. [164] {And now that we understand all the passions, we have much less reason to fear them than we had before. For we see that they are all good in their nature, and that we have nothing to avoid but their misuse or their

---

159. Art. 209. *Regret.*

160. Art. 210. *Cheerfulness.*

161. Original text: follow the order of enumeration I did above; but it seems to me that this enumeration has been useful in showing that we have not omitted any that were worthy of any special consideration.

162. From Art. 147. *The internal emotions of the soul.*

163. Omitted: which, as it sometimes happens, he would be sorry to see her brought back to life again, it can happen that his heart is gripped by the sadness excited in him by the funeral display and the absence of a person whose company he was accustomed to; and it can happen that some remnants of love or pity present themselves to his imagination and draw real tears from his eyes.

164. From Art. 211. *A general remedy against the passions*; Art. 212. *The good and evil of this life depends on passions alone* is omitted.

excesses, against which the remedies I explained might suffice if everyone took enough care to apply them.} [. . .] The most general and most easily applicable *remedy* against all the excesses of the passions, is that, when we feel our blood thus agitated, we should take heed and remember that everything presented to the imagination tends to mislead the soul and make the reasons for pursuing the object of its passion appear much stronger than they are, and those for dissuading it from that pursuit much weaker.

[487]

[165] <The *function* of the passions> is to induce the soul to consent and contribute to actions that may serve to preserve the body or to make it in some way more perfect. [166]But, even though this function of the passions is the most natural they can have, [. . .] nevertheless, it is not always good, as there are many things harmful to the body that do not cause any initial sadness or even impart joy, and other things beneficial to it. That is why we must make use of experience and reason, and not allow ourselves to do anything in excess.

[430]

[431]

---

165. From Art. 137. *The function of the five passions is explained here, insofar as they relate to the body.*
166. From Art. 138. *Their defects and the means for correcting them.*

Chapter III

What Is Love?[1]

There are two kinds of love, purely *intellectual* or *sensitive* love, which is a passion.[2] The *first*, it seems to me, is nothing other than when our soul perceives some present or absent good it judges to be suitable for itself, it attaches itself to it willingly, that is, it considers itself and the good as a whole of which it and the good are two parts. Then, if the good is present, that is, if the soul possesses it, or is possessed by it, or is joined to it not merely through its will but also really, and in fact, and in the way it is suitable for it to be joined, the motion of the will accompanying the knowledge it has that this would be good for it is joy; and if it is absent, the motion of the will accompanying the knowledge it has of being deprived of it is sadness; but the one accompanying the knowledge it has that it would be good for it to acquire is desire. And all these motions {of the will} in which love, {joy, sadness, and desire} consist, insofar as they are rational thoughts and not passions, could be found in our soul even if it had no body. {For example, if the soul perceived that there are many very beautiful things to know in nature, its will would infallibly lead it to love the knowledge of these things, that is, to consider such knowledge as belonging to it. And if it noticed with this, that it had this knowledge, it would be joyful. If it considered that it did not have it, it would be sad. If it thought that it would be good for it to acquire it, it would desire it. And there is nothing in all these motions of its will which would be obscure to it, or anything of which it could not have a very perfect knowledge, provided it reflected on its own thoughts. But while our soul is joined to our body, this rational love is typically accompanied by the other kind of love, which we can call sensual or sensuous. And, as I said briefly of all the passions, appetites, and sensations, on page 461 of my French-language *Principles* [*Principles* IV, Art. 189–90]}, *sensitive* love is nothing other than a confused thought

---

1. From Descartes to Chanut (February 1, 1647), AT IV, 601–6, Clerselier/*Epistolae* Letter 35.

2. Original sentence: I distinguish between love which is purely intellectual or rational and love which is a passion.

brought about in the soul by some motion of the nerves, disposing it to this other, clearer thought in which consists rational love. {Just as in thirst the sensation we have of dryness in the throat is a confused thought inclining to the desire to drink, but it is not the same as this desire, likewise in love we feel a vague heat near the heart and a great abundance of blood in the lungs that even makes us open our arms as if to embrace something and inclines the soul to join itself willingly with the object presented. But the thought by which the soul feels this heat is different from the one joining it to this object; it even sometimes happens that this feeling of love arises in us without our will being led to love anything, because we do not encounter any object that we deem worthy of it. It can also happen, in contrast, that we are acquainted with some very deserving good and we willingly join ourselves to it without having any passion for that, because the body is not disposed to it.}

Ordinarily, these two loves occur together; for there is such a connection between them that, when the soul judges an object to be worthy of it, it immediately disposes the heart toward the motions exciting the passion of love; and when the heart finds itself thus disposed by other causes, it makes the soul imagine loveable qualities in objects where previously it only saw defects. And it is no wonder that certain motions of the heart are so naturally joined to certain thoughts to which they have no resemblance; for, from the fact that our soul is of such a nature that it was able to be united with a body, it also has the property that each of its thoughts can so strongly associate with certain motions or dispositions of this body such that, when the same dispositions are found in it at some other time, they induce the soul to the same thought; and conversely, {when the same thought recurs, it prepares the body to receive the same disposition. Thus, when we learn a language, we connect the letters or pronunciation of certain words, which are material things, with their significations, which are thoughts. Afterward, when we once again hear the same words, we conceive the same things; and when we conceive the same things, we remember the same words}.

But the first dispositions of the body which thus accompanied our thoughts, when we first entered the world, must no doubt have been connected more closely with them than those accompanying them afterward. {To examine the origin of the heat we feel around the heart and those of the other dispositions of the body accompanying love, I consider that, from the first moment our soul was joined to the body, it probably felt joy, and love immediately after, then perhaps also hatred and sadness; and the same dispositions of the body which then caused these passions afterward naturally accompanied the corresponding thoughts.} I judge that the soul's first passion was *joy*, because it is not credible that the soul was put in the body except when it was well-disposed, and that, when it is thus well-disposed this naturally gives us joy. {I also say that} *love* came after joy, because the matter of our bodies is constantly in flux, like the water in a river, and there is a need for new matter to replace the old, so it is hardly likely that the body would have been well-disposed had there not been nearby it some matter suitable to serve as nourishment for it; the soul, willingly uniting itself to this new matter, must have felt love for it; if nourishment was lacking, the soul must have felt *sadness*; if its place was taken by some unsuitable matter, the soul must have felt *hatred* toward it.[3]

These are the four passions I believe to have been first in us, and the only ones we had before our birth; and I also believe they were at that time only sensations or very confused thoughts: {the soul was so attached to matter that it could not yet attend to anything else but to receive different impressions from it; and although, some years later, it may have begun to have other joys and other loves than those depending only on the good constitution and suitable nourishment of the body, nevertheless, the intellectual component of its joys or loves was always accompanied by the first sensations it had of them, and even by the motions or natural functions present in the body at such times; thus, to the extent love was only caused, before birth, by suitable food, which, entering abundantly in the liver, the heart, and the lungs, produced more heat there than normal, as a result it is now the case that this heat always accompanies love, even though it now comes from very different causes. If I was not afraid of going on too long, I could show in detail that all the other dispositions of the body there at the beginning of our lives with these four passions still accompany them}. I will simply say that these confused sensations of our childhood, which, remaining joined to the rational thoughts by which we love what we judge worthy, are the reason the nature of love is difficult for us to know. {To this I add that several other passions, such as joy, sadness, desire, fear, hope, etc., by mixing differently with love, prevent us from recognizing what it properly consists in. This is especially noticeable with respect to desire,

---

3. Original sentence: and later, if it happened that this nourishment was lacking, the soul must have felt sadness. And, if its place was taken by some other matter that was not proper to nourish the body, the soul must have felt hatred toward it.

for} we take desire for love so often that we distinguish two sorts of love: one, benevolent, in which this desire is not very prominent; and the other, concupiscent, which is only a very violent desire, based on a love that is often weak.[4]

Whether Natural Light Alone Teaches Us to Love God?[5]

\<There are\> two strong reasons for doubting this. The first is that the attributes of God {we consider most commonly} are so high above us that we do not conceive in any way how they can be suitable for us, which is the reason we do not join ourselves to them willingly. The second is that there is nothing imaginable in God, which makes it such that although we would have an intellectual love for him, it does not seem that we could have any such sensible love, because it would have to pass through the imagination in order to come from the understanding into the senses. {This is why I am not surprised if some philosophers are convinced that only the Christian religion, by teaching us the mystery of the Incarnation, by which God lowered himself to the point of becoming similar to us, makes us capable of loving him; those who, without the knowledge of this mystery, seemed to have passion for some divinity, did not, as a result, have any for the true God, but only for some idols they called by his name—in the same way as the poets say that Ixion embraced a cloud instead of the Queen of the Gods.} Yet I do not doubt that we can truly love God by the sole power of our nature. {I do not assert that this love is meritorious without grace; I leave the theologians to sort that out. But I dare say that, as regards this life, it is the most delightful and most useful passion we could have; and it can even be the strongest, although, for that, we need a very attentive meditation, because we are constantly distracted by the presence of other objects.} Now, the path I judge we must follow to reach the love of God is to consider that he is a mind, or a thing that thinks. Since the nature of our soul bears some resemblance to his, we come to persuade ourselves

IV, 607

608

---

4. Original sentence: for we take it for love so often that we are led to distinguish two sorts of love: one, which we call benevolent love, in which this desire is not very prominent; and the other, which we call concupiscent love, which is only a very violent desire, based on a love which is often weak.
5. From Descartes to Chanut (February 1, 1647), AT IV, 607–13, Clerselier/*Epistolae* Letter 35.

that it is an emanation of his supreme intelligence, *almost a breath of the divine wind*.⁶ {Further, since our knowledge seems to be able to increase by degrees to infinity and God's knowledge being infinite is the end toward which ours aims, if we consider nothing more, we can arrive at the extravagance of wanting to be gods, and thus, through a very great error, love only divinity instead of loving God.} But in addition, we must take heed of the infinity of his power, by which he created so many things of which we are but the smallest part. And we must consider the extent of his providence {which makes it that he sees with a single thought all that was, is, will be, and would have been}. Add to this the infallibility of his decrees {which, although they do not interfere with our free will, could nevertheless not be changed in any way. And finally, we must consider, on the one hand}, our smallness, and {on the other, the greatness of all created things, noting how they depend on God and regarding them in a way that relates them to his omnipotence, without enclosing them in a ball, as do those who want the world to be finite}. A meditation on all these things fills a person who understands them well with a joy so extreme that, {far from being insulting and ungrateful to God to the point of wanting to take his place, he thinks he has already lived amply from God's having given him the grace to arrive at such knowledge. Joining himself willingly to God,} he loves him so perfectly and no longer desires anything more in the world, except that God's will should be done. {As a result, he no longer fears death, pain, or disgrace, because he knows that nothing can happen to him except what God has decreed; and he so loves this divine decree, esteems it to be so just and so necessary, and knows he must entirely depend upon it. Even when he expects death or some other ill as its outcome, if, against all possibility, he could change it, he would not will to do so. But if he does not reject illnesses or afflictions because they come from divine providence, he rejects even less all the licit goods and pleasures he may enjoy in this life, since they too come from God; he receives them with joy and without any fear of ill.} <Thus, it will happen that, amidst his own adversity or prosperity,> his love makes him perfectly happy.

{It is true that the soul must strongly detach itself from association with the senses to represent to itself the truths arousing this love in it; thus, it seems that it cannot communicate this love to the faculty of imagination, so as to make it a passion. But, nevertheless, I do not doubt that it

---

6. Horace, *Satires* II. 2, v. 79.

does communicate it.} Although we cannot imagine anything of what is in God, who is the object of our love, we can imagine our love itself, which consists in wanting to unite ourselves with some object. With respect to God this is to consider ourselves as a very small part of the immensity of things he has created; given the diversity of objects, we can unite or join with them in different ways; and the idea of this union alone suffices to excite the heat around the heart and cause a very violent passion.

It is true as well that {the use of our language and} the civility of compliments allows us only to say to those whose condition is very far above ours that we respect them, {honor, and esteem them, and that we are zealous and devoted to their service,} but not that we *love* them; {this seems to me the reason that} friendship between people {when it is reciprocal} in some sense makes them equals. [. . .] <Philosophers pay no regard to these things;> and far from the love we have for objects above us being less than the love we have for others, I believe that, by its nature, this love is more perfect and makes us more strongly embrace the interests of what we love. <For, to the extent that the whole, of which we are but a part, is most precious, we take it up with great intensity.> [. . .] As a result, it is evident that our love for God must be without comparison the greatest and most perfect of all.

What Are the Causes Often Inciting Us to Love Someone in Preference to Another before We Know His Merit?[7]

<There are two causes for this,> one of which is in the mind and the other in the body. But as for the one only in the mind, it presupposes so many things concerning the nature of our souls that I should not dare to undertake <them here>. I will speak only of the one in the body. It consists in the disposition of the parts of our brain, whether that disposition was placed there by the objects of the senses, or by some other cause. For the objects touching our senses move some parts of our brain through the mediation of the nerves, and make, as it were, some folds there, which are unfolded when the object stops acting. But the part where they were made afterward remains disposed to be folded again in the

---

7. From Descartes to Chanut (June 6, 1647), AT V, 56–58, Clerselier/*Epistolae* Letter 36.

same way by another object that somehow resembles the former object, even if it does not resemble it in everything. {For example, when I was a child, I loved a girl of my age who was slightly cross-eyed. As a result, the impression made by my sight in my brain when I looked at her wayward eyes became so closely linked to what aroused in me the passion of love, that for a long time afterward, when I saw cross-eyed people, I felt more inclined to love them than to love others, just because they had that defect. Nevertheless, I did not know this was the reason. On the other hand, after I reflected on it, and recognized that it was a deficiency, I was no longer moved by it.} Thus, when we are moved to love someone without knowing the cause, we may believe that it arises from something in the person similar to what was in another object we previously loved, without our knowing what it was. And although it is usually a perfection rather than a defect which thus attracts us to love, still, since it can sometimes be a defect, {as in the example I mentioned,} a wise man must not give in entirely to this passion before he has considered the merit of the person for whom he feels moved. But since we cannot love equally all those in whom we find equal merit, I believe we are only obliged to esteem them equally. {And since the chief good of life is to have affection for some, we are right to prefer those to whom our secret inclinations unite us, provided we also observe in them some merit. Further,} when our secret inclinations have their cause in the mind, and not in the body, I believe they should always be followed. And the chief mark that makes them known is that those that come from the mind are reciprocal, which does not happen often to the others.

Which of Two Disorders Is Worse, That of Love or That of Hatred?[8]

This question can be understood in different ways, {which it seems to me need to be examined separately}. We can say that a passion is worse than another because it makes us less virtuous, or because it is more repugnant to our contentment, or again because it leads us to greater excesses and disposes us to do more harm to other men.

---

8. From Descartes to Chanut (February 1, 1647), AT IV, 613–17, Clerselier/*Epistolae* Letter 35.

Chapter III

{As for the first point, I find it doubtful. For} considering the definitions of these two passions, I judge that loving an undeserving object can be worse for us than hating another we should love: there is more danger in being joined to a bad thing, and being as it were transformed through it, than there is in being separated willingly from a good thing. But when I pay heed to the inclinations or habits arising from these passions, I change my mind. Love, {however deranged it may be,} always has the good as its object; it seems to me that it cannot corrupt our morals as much as hatred, which only recommends evil. {We see by experience that the best people become gradually malicious when they are obliged to hate someone; for, even though their hatred is just, they focus so often on the evils they receive from their enemy and those they wish him, that this gradually accustoms them to malice. By contrast, those who devote themselves to loving, even if their love is deranged and frivolous, often do not fail to become more honest and virtuous.} <Even when hatred is just, it gradually accustoms people to malice; on the other hand, with inordinate love one can emerge as a better person> than if one's mind were given to other thoughts.

As for the second point, I find no difficulty with it. Hatred is always accompanied by sadness and grief. {Whatever pleasure some people take in doing harm to others, I believe that their pleasure is similar to that of demons who, according to our religion, do not escape damnation, even though they imagine themselves as constantly seeking vengeance against God by tormenting people in Hell.} Love, on the contrary, however deranged it might be, gives pleasure; {and although the poets often complain about it in their verses, I nevertheless believe that people would naturally refrain from loving if they did not find in it more sweetness than bitterness}. All the afflictions to which we attribute love as cause come only from other passions accompanying it, namely, reckless desires and ill-founded hopes.

But if we ask which of these two passions leads us to greater excess and makes us capable of doing more harm to other people, it seems to me to be love, especially since it naturally has much more power and vigor than hatred. [. . .] <This is proven> through their origins, [. . .] that is, blood, in love sends more animal spirits to the brain than hatred. [. . .] It is also proven through experience; {for the Hercules, the Rolands, and} generally those with the most courage love more ardently than others; and inversely, the weak and cowardly are more inclined toward hatred. Anger can make men bold, but it borrows its strength from the love we have for ourselves, which always serves as its foundation, and not from the hatred that only accompanies it. Despair also inspires great exercises in courage, and fear leads to great cruelty; but there is a difference between these passions and hatred. {It remains for me to prove that the love we have for an object of little importance can cause more harm, when deranged, than does hatred of another one of more value. And the reason I give for this is that} the harm arising from hatred extends only to the hated object, whereas deranged love spares nothing except its object, {which is typically so small in comparison with all the other things whose loss and ruin it is prepared to bring about,} for these to serve as food for the extravagance of its fury. It might be said that hatred is the proximate cause of the evils attributed to love, because if we love something, by the same means we hate everything contrary to it. But love is always more to blame than hatred for the evils that transpire in this way, especially since it is the first cause, and the love of a single object can thus give rise to hatred for many others. Furthermore, the greatest evils of love are not those it commits in this way, through the intermediary of hatred; the chief and most dangerous ones are those done, or allowed to be done, simply for the pleasure of the loved object, or for our own.

The Joy of the Soul[9]

IV, 529   As the health of the body and the presence of agreeable objects greatly help the mind to chase from itself all the passions that participate in sadness, and to grant entrance to those that participate in joy, thus, reciprocally, when the mind is full of joy, this serves very much to make the body more fit {and present objects to appear more agreeable. And I even also dare to believe that} internal joy has some secret power to make fortune more favorable.[10] The experiences I have often noticed are that the things I did with a happy heart, and without any internal repugnance, usually succeeded happily for me, even to the point at which, in games of chance, where

---

9. From Descartes to Elisabeth [November 1646], AT IV, 529–30, Clerselier/*Epistolae* Letter 15.

10. Omitted: I would not want to write this to people with weak minds, for fear of inducing some superstition in them; but, regarding your Highness, I only fear that she laughs at seeing me become too credulous. However, I have an infinity of experiences, and with them the authority of Socrates, to confirm my opinion.

there is but fortune alone that reigns, I always felt it more favorable when I had cause for joy than when I had cause for sadness.[11] But, concerning the important actions in life, when they happen to be so doubtful that prudence cannot teach what must be done, it seems to me that we have strong reasons for following the advice of our own daemon [inner voice], and that it is useful to have a strong belief that the things we <happily> undertake {without repugnance and with the freedom that typically accompanies joy,} will not fail to succeed for us.

Whether It Is Better to Be Joyful and Content, Imagining the Goods We Possess to Be Greater and More Valuable Than They Are, Than to Have More Consideration and Knowledge, and Know the Right Value of Both and Thus to Grow Sadder?[12]

If I thought the supreme good was joy, I would not doubt that we must try to render ourselves joyful at any price whatever, and I would approve the brutishness of those who drown their displeasures in wine or dull them with tobacco. But I make a distinction between the supreme good that consists in the exercise of virtue {or what is the same, in the possession of all those goods whose acquisition depends upon our free will,} and the satisfaction of mind that results from that acquisition. That is why, seeing that it is a greater perfection to know the truth than to be ignorant of it, even when it is to our disadvantage, I confess that it is better to be less joyful and have more knowledge. So, it is not always the most joyful person who has the most satisfied mind; on the contrary, great joys are commonly sober and serious, and only slight and passing ones are accompanied by laughter. Thus, I cannot approve of our trying to deceive ourselves by

---

11. Omitted: And what one commonly calls Socrates's daemon was without doubt nothing other than that he had accustomed himself to follow its internal inclinations and thought that the outcome of what he was undertaking would be happy when he had some secret feeling of cheerfulness, and, inversely, that it would be unhappy when he was sad. It is true, however, that it would be superstitious to believe this as much as it is said he did; for Plato reports [Plato, *Apology* 31d] that he even remained in his home whenever his daemon did not advise him to leave it.

12. From Descartes to Elisabeth (October 6, 1645), AT IV, 305–9, Clerselier/*Epistolae* Letter 8.

feeding ourselves false imaginations. {For the pleasure resulting from this can only touch the surface of the soul, which however senses an internal bitterness when it perceives that they are false. And yet it could happen that the soul was so continually diverted that it never perceived it; but we would not in this way enjoy the happiness in question, because it must depend on our conduct, and in the latter case it could come only from fortune.} But when it is possible for us to have different considerations that are equally true, ones leading to being content and others, conversely, preventing it, it seems to me that prudence demands that we stop chiefly with those giving us satisfaction. [. . .] <I do not see> why there is subject for regret for having done what we judged to be best at the time we needed to decide to act, even though later, thinking it over at our leisure, we decide we were mistaken. {But we should rather regret if we did something against our conscience, even though we recognized afterward that we did better than we thought. For we answer only for our thoughts, and human nature is not omniscient, or always able to judge as well on the spot as when we have plenty of time to deliberate.} Besides, the vanity that causes us to have a better opinion of ourselves than we should is a vice belonging only to weak and base souls; but this does not mean that the strongest and most noble souls must despise themselves. We must do justice to ourselves and recognize our perfections as well as our faults; and if politeness prevents us from broadcasting them, it does not prevent us from being aware of them. [. . .] It is easy to prove that the pleasure of the soul constituting happiness is not inseparable from the joyfulness and comfort of the body. For example, tragedies please us more as they incite greater sadness in us, and physical exercises {like hunting, tennis, and other such things} are pleasant despite their being arduous; indeed, we see that often fatigue and discomfort increase pleasure. The cause of the contentment that the soul derives from such exercises consists in that it is made aware of the strength, or skill, or some other perfection of the body to which it is joined; but the contentment it receives in weeping, when seeing[13] some tragedy, arises mainly from its thinking that it acts virtuously when having compassion for the afflicted. In general, the soul is pleased {to feel the passions being incited in it, no matter what their nature,} as long as it retains a mastery of those passions.

---

13. Original phrase: some pitiable and tragic episode being represented in the theater.

Appendix

The Provisional Morals[1]

And in the end, as it is not enough, before starting to rebuild the house in which we live, to tear it down, and to provide materials and architects, or practice architecture ourselves, and in addition, to have a carefully drawn plan, but we must also have some other place where we can be comfortably housed during the work; thus, in order that I would not remain irresolute in my actions, while reason compelled me to be so in my judgments and I could still live as happily as I could, I formed a provisional code of morals, consisting only of three or four maxims, which I would like to share with you.

The first was to obey the laws and customs of my country, adhering constantly to the religion in which, by the grace of God, I was instructed from my childhood, and governing myself in all other ways according to the most moderate opinions, those farthest removed from excess, that were commonly accepted in practice by the most judicious of those with whom I would have to live. For, starting henceforth to count my own opinions as nothing, because I wanted to subject them all to examination, I was certain I could not do better than to follow those of the most judicious. And although there may be people among the Persians or the Chinese just as judicious as among ourselves, it seemed to me that the most useful thing was to rule myself according to those with whom I would have to live; and, in order to know what their opinions truly were, I had to be aware of what they practiced rather than what they said, not only because, in the corruption of our customs, few people are willing to say everything they believe, but also because many do not themselves know what they believe: the action of thought by which one believes something being different from the one by which one knows one believes it, they are often without one another. And, among several opinions equally acceptable, I chose only the most moderate, not only because they are always the most practically

---
1. *Discourse on Method,* Part III (1637), AT VI, 22–31.

convenient and likely the best (all excesses usually being bad), but also to divert me less from the true path, in case I should fail, than if, having chosen one of the extremes, it should have been the other I needed to follow. And I specifically placed among the extremes all the promises whereby something of our freedom is curtailed—not that I would disapprove of laws, which, in order to remedy the instability of weak minds, permit, when someone has a good purpose or even, for the security of commerce, a merely indifferent purpose, to execute vows or contracts that require perseverance—but because I saw nothing in the world always remaining in the same state, and because, for my part, I promised myself to perfect my judgments more and more, and not at all to make them worse; thus, I would have thought myself to be committing a great fault against common sense if, because I once approved of something, I would have been obliged to regard it as good again afterward, when it might have stopped being so or I might have stopped considering it as such.

My second maxim was to be as firm and resolute in my actions as I could, and to follow no less steadfastly the most dubious opinions, once I had decided on them, than if they had been once very certain. In this I would be imitating the travelers, who, finding themselves lost in some forest, must not err by wandering around, sometimes turning to one side and sometimes to another, let alone stopping in one place, but always walking as straight as they can in one direction, and never changing it for weak reasons, although at the start chance alone may have been what determined them to choose it; for, by this means, if they do not go exactly where they want, at least in the end they will arrive somewhere where they will likely be better off than in the middle of a forest. And thus, since the actions of life often do not suffer any delay, it is a very certain truth that, when it is not in our power to discern the truest opinions, we must follow the most probable; and even though we do not observe any more likelihood in some than in others, we must nevertheless settle on some, and consider them afterward no longer as dubious as they relate to practice, but as very true and very certain, because the reason that made us determine this finds it to be so. And this henceforth was able to free me from all the regret and remorse that usually stir the consciences of those weak and irresolute minds who constantly indulge in treating things as good that they later deem to be bad.

My third maxim was always to try to conquer myself rather than fortune, and to change my desires rather than the order of the world, and in general, to accustom myself to believing that there is nothing entirely in our power except our thoughts, so that after we did our best concerning things external to us, the only thing lacking for us to succeed is, with respect to us, absolutely impossible. And this alone seemed to me sufficient to prevent me from desiring anything in the future that I could not acquire, and thus render me contented; for, since our will naturally only comes to desire the things our understanding represents to it as possible in some way, it is certain that if we consider all the goods external to us as equally beyond our power, we will no more regret the lacking of those that seem to be due to our birth, when deprived of them without any fault of ours, than our not possessing the kingdoms of China or Mexico—making, as they say, a virtue of necessity, we will no more desire being healthy when sick, or being free when in prison, than we now do of having bodies of a matter as incorruptible as diamonds, or wings to fly like birds. But I admit that there is need for long exercise and frequently repeated meditation, to get used to looking at all things from this perspective; and I believe that it is principally in this that the secret of these philosophers consisted, who were once able to escape from the dominion of fortune, and, despite pain and poverty, could debate about happiness with their gods. For, constantly taking care to consider the limits prescribed to them by nature, they persuaded themselves so perfectly that nothing was in their power but their thoughts, that this alone was sufficient to prevent them from having any affection for other things; and they disposed of their thoughts so absolutely that they had on this account a reason for considering themselves richer and more powerful, freer and happier than other people who, however favored by nature and fortune they might be, if lacking this philosophy, can never command the realization of everything they want.

    Finally, to conclude this morality, I resolved to review the various occupations people have in this life, in order to try to choose the best one; and, without wanting to say anything about the occupations of others, I thought that I could not do better than to continue in the very one in which I found myself, that is, to use my whole life to cultivate my reason and advance as much as I could in the knowledge of the truth, following the method I prescribed myself. I experienced such extreme contentment since I began to use this method, that I did not believe one could receive any sweeter or more innocent contentment in this life; and, discovering every day by its means some truths that seemed to me quite important and commonly not known by other people, the satisfaction I derived from it filled my mind so much that nothing else concerned me. Moreover, the three previous maxims were based only on the intention I had to continue to teach myself; for God having given each of us some light to discern the true from the false, I would not have thought I had to be content with the opinions of others for a single moment, had I not proposed to myself to use my own judgment to examine them when there would be time. And I would not have been able to free myself of scruples in following them, had I thought I would lose any opportunity of finding better ones, in case there were any. And finally, I would not have been able to limit my desires or be content, had I not followed a path by which, thinking I would be certain of acquiring all the knowledge I would be capable of, I thought I would be certain by the same means of acquiring all the real goods that would be ever in my power. Inasmuch as our will does not seek to follow or shun anything except insofar as our understanding represents it as good or bad, it is enough to judge well to do well, and to judge as best we can to do as best as possible, that is, to acquire all the virtues and together all the other goods we can acquire; and when we are sure that this is the case, we cannot fail to be content.

Having thus assured myself of these maxims and placed them apart with the truths of faith, which always occupied the first place in my belief, I judged that I could freely undertake to get rid of the rest of my opinions. And because I hoped to be able to succeed better by conversing with people than by staying longer confined to the stove-heated room where I had all these thoughts, I began to travel again when winter was not yet completely over. And in all the next nine years I did nothing but roam around the world, going here and there, trying to be a spectator rather than an actor in all the comedies that are played out there; and, reflecting purposely on each matter about what might make it suspect and give us an occasion for error, I uprooted from my mind all the errors that previously were able to slip into it. Not that I imitated for this the skeptics, who doubt only to doubt, and affect to be always undecided; for, on the contrary, my whole purpose tended only to assure myself, and to cast aside loose earth and sand that I might reach rock or clay. It seems to me I was quite successful, to the extent that, trying to discover the falsity or uncertainty of the propositions I was examining, not by weak conjecture, but by clear and certain reasoning, I encountered none so dubious that I could not always draw some quite certain conclusion, even if it was just that it contained nothing certain. And, just as in knocking down an old dwelling, the wreckage is usually reserved to serve in building a new one, so, by destroying all those of my opinions I judged to be poorly founded, I made various observations and acquired several experiences that have since served me in establishing more certain ones. Moreover, I continued to practice the method I prescribed for myself; for, in addition to taking care of generally conducting all my thoughts according to its rules, I reserved a few hours, from time to time, that I used specifically to practice mathematical problems, or even also others I could turn into problems fairly similar to those of mathematics, by detaching them from all the principles of the other sciences that I did not find firm enough, as you will see I did in many of them explained in this volume.[2] And so, without living in appearance in any way other than those who, having no vocation other than spending a sweet and innocent life, studying to separate pleasures from vices, and who, in order to enjoy their leisure without boredom, use all honest diversions, I did not fail to pursue my project and to profit in the knowledge of the truth, perhaps more than if I had only read books or frequented people of letters.

However, these nine years passed before I had as yet taken any part in the issues that are commonly contested between the learned or begun to seek the foundations of any philosophy more certain than the common one. And the example of several excellent minds who previously engaged with such a project, but it seems without success, made me imagine so much difficulty in it that I might not have dared to undertake it any time soon, had I not heard that some people were already spreading the rumor that I had succeeded in my endeavor. I cannot say on what they based their opinion; and if my discourses contributed anything to this, it must have been because I admitted my ignorance more freely than those who studied only a little are accustomed to doing, and perhaps also because I showed the reasons that I had for doubting many things others consider as certain, rather than because I boasted of possessing any doctrine. But having a good enough heart not to want to be taken for anything other than what I was, I thought I had to try by every means to render myself worthy of the reputation I was given; and exactly eight years ago this desire made me resolve to move away from all the places where I might have acquaintances, and to withdraw here, to a country where the long duration of war led to the

---

2. Descartes published the *Discourse on Method* in a single volume with the *Dioptrics, Meteors,* and *Geometry,* three essays which, in the title of the volume, are said to be "samples of the method."

establishment of such order that the armies maintained there seem only to enable people to enjoy the fruits of peace with greater security, and where, among the crowd of a great and quite active people, more careful of their own affairs than curious about those of others, without lacking any of the conveniences to be found in the most frequented cities, I was able to live a life as solitary and withdrawn as in the most remote deserts.

Two Questions about the Provisional Morals

From S. P. to [Reneri] for Descartes [April 1638][3]

I, 512 Not daring to address Mr. Descartes directly to propose my difficulties to him, I borrow your influence to ask you to present them and to try to ensure that he would receive them well, as coming from a person who has more desire to learn than to contradict.

513 First, the second rule of his morals[4] seems to be dangerous, maintaining that we must hold the opinions we once determined to follow when they would be most doubtful, just as if they were the most certain; for if they are false or bad, the more we follow them, the more we would be engaged in error or vice.

2. The third rule[5] is rather a fiction to flatter and deceive ourselves than the resolution of a philosopher, who must despise possible things, if it is expedient for him, without pretending them to be impossible; and a person of common sense can never persuade himself that nothing is in his power but his thoughts.

From Descartes to [Reneri] for S. P. [May 1638][6]

II, 34 There was no need for your friend to be so ceremonious. Those of his merit and his mind do not need intermediaries, and I will always take it as a favor when people such as him want to do the honor of consulting me regarding my writings. I ask you to remove this contingency from him, but this time, because he wanted it, I will take the trouble to address my replies to him through you.

---

3. AT I, 512–13.
4. AT VI, 24–25.
5. AT VI, 25–27.
6. AT II, 34–37.

First, it is true that, if I said absolutely that we must hold to the opinions we once determined to follow, even though they are doubtful, I would not be any less reprehensible than if I said we must be opinionated and obstinate—because holding to an opinion is the same as remaining in the judgment we made of it. But I said something completely different, namely, that we must be resolute in our actions, while we remain irresolute in our judgments (see p. 24, line 8),[7] and not follow any less constantly the most doubtful opinions, in other words, not act less constantly following the opinions we judge to be doubtful, when we have once determined to do so. By this I meant that, when we consider that there are no others we judge to be better or more certain, rather than if we knew that those were the best—as, in fact, these are so under this condition (see p. 26, line 15).[8] And there is no need to fear that this firmness in action sets us further and further into error or vice, insofar as error can only be in the understanding, which I am supposing, despite this, to remain free and consider as doubtful that which is doubtful. Further, I only apply this rule to actions in life that admit of no delay and only use this provisionally (p. 24, line 10),[9] with the intent to change my opinions as soon as I can find better ones, and not to miss any opportunity in searching for them (p. 29, line 8).[10] Moreover, I was obliged to speak of this resolution and firmness regarding action as much because it is necessary for ease of conscience as for preventing others blaming me for writing that to avoid preconception we must once in our life undo all the opinions we believed before. Otherwise, people would have objected that such a universal doubt can produce great irresolution and great moral chaos. It seems to me I could not have been more cautious than if I were to place resolution, insofar as it is a virtue, between the two vices contrary to it: namely, indecision and obstinacy.

2. It does not seem to me a fiction, but a truth that must not be denied by anyone, that there is nothing entirely in our power other than our thoughts. At the least, taking the word thought as I do, for all the operations of the soul, such that, not only meditations and volitions, but also the functions of sight, hearing, and determining ourselves toward

---

7. AT VI, 22.
8. AT VI, 25.
9. AT VI, 22.
10. AT VI, 27.

one motion rather than another, etc., insofar as they depend on the soul, are thoughts. There is absolutely nothing more than the things comprised under this word that we attribute properly to humans in the language of philosophers: as for the functions belonging solely to the body, we say they are in humans, not by humans. Moreover, the word "entirely" (p. 27, line 3),[11] and what follows it, namely, when we did our best regarding external things, everything we fail to achieve is "absolutely" impossible with regards to us. I state sufficiently that I did not want to say, for this, that external things were not at all in our power, but they are in our power only insofar as they can follow from our thoughts, and not "absolutely" nor "entirely," because there are other powers outside of us that can prevent the effects of our designs. To express this better, I connected these two expressions together: "with regards to us and absolutely," which the critics could take as contradicting each other, except that the understanding of their meanings allows it. Now, no external thing is in our power, insofar as it depends on the direction of our soul, and there is absolutely nothing in our power other than our thoughts. Although this is quite true, and it seems to me no one could find a difficulty in accepting this when he thinks about it expressly, I say however that it is necessary to accustom ourselves to believing it, and even that a long exercise and often-repeated meditation is needed for this effect. This is because our appetites and our passions continually tell us the opposite, and we experienced so many times since our childhood that in crying, or commanding, etc., we make ourselves obeyed by our nurses and obtained the things we wanted, that we are insensibly persuaded the world is made for us alone and everything is owed to us. In this, those who are born great and fortunate have more opportunities to be mistaken; we can also see that it is these people who ordinarily endure most impatiently the ignominies of fortune. But there is not, it seems to me, a more worthy occupation for a philosopher than to accustom himself to believing what true reason tells him, and to guard himself against the false opinions his natural appetites urge upon him.

---

11. AT VI, 25.

The Longevity of Life and Morals[12]

I would have to be very tired of living if I neglected to look after myself after reading your last letter. You tell me in it that you and some other people of very great merit were so concerned about me that you feared I was ill, when two weeks passed without your receiving a letter from me. But thank God, I did not have any illness for the last thirty years that would deserve to be called serious. Besides, age took away that warmth of the liver that once caused me to love the military and I no longer profess anything but lack of courage; I also acquired some small knowledge of medicine and I feel well and look after myself with as much care as a rich man with gout. Thus, it almost seems to me I am now further from death than I was in my youth. And if God does not grant me enough knowledge to avoid the inconveniences that age brings, I hope he will leave me at least enough time in this life that I may have the leisure to endure them. However, everything depends upon his providence, to which, pleasantry aside, I submit myself with as much good heart as Father Joseph[13] could have done; and one of the points of my morals is to love life without fearing death.

II, 480

From the Letters by Elisabeth to Descartes
Elisabeth to Descartes (August 16 [1645])[14]

I still do not know if I can rid myself of doubt as to whether the happiness of which you speak can be attained without the assistance of things that do not depend absolutely on the will. For there are illnesses that completely take away our ability to reason and, consequently, that of enjoying rational satisfaction. And there are others that diminish its strength and prevent us from following the maxims good sense would have forged, that make the most moderate people subject to being carried away by their passions and less capable of handling the accidents of fortune that require prompt resolution. When Epicurus, beset by kidney stones, struggled to assure his friends that he felt no pain, instead of screaming like common people, he

IV, 269

---
12. From a Letter to Mersenne (January 9, 1639), AT II, 480.
13. François Joseph Le Clerc du Tremblay, a Capuchin, who died on December 18, 1638, at the age of sixty-one.
14. AT IV, 269–70.

led the life of a philosopher, not that of a prince, captain, or courtier, and he knew that nothing external would happen to him to make him forget his role and fail to resolve the problem according to the rules of his philosophy. It is on these occasions that regret seems inevitable to me, and the knowledge that failing is as natural to a person as being sick cannot protect us from it. For we also are not unaware of the fact that we could exempt ourselves from each specific fault.

But I am sure you will enlighten me about these difficulties, and many more of which I am not now aware, when you teach me the truths that must be known in order to facilitate the exercise of virtue. Therefore, please do not forget your plan of obliging me with your precepts and know that I esteem them as much as they deserve it.

Elisabeth to Descartes (September 13 [1645])[15]

If my conscience remained satisfied with the pretexts you give as remedies to my ignorance, I would be much obliged to it and would be exempt from the need for regret for having so poorly used the time in which I enjoyed the use of reason; this was a longer period than others of my age, since my birth and my fortune forced me at an early age to use my judgment for the conduct of a rather arduous life, free from the prosperities that could prevent me from thinking about myself, such as the subjection that would have required me to rely on the prudence of a governess.

It is not, however, these prosperities, nor the flatteries that accompany them, that I believe absolutely capable of removing the strength of mind from well-born souls and preventing them from receiving a change of fortune as a philosopher. But I am persuaded that the multitude of accidents that surprise the people governing the public, without giving them the time to examine the most useful solution, often leads them (however virtuous they may be) to take actions that later cause them to regret, which you say is one of the principal obstacles to beatitude.[16] It is true that a habit of estimating goods according to whether they can contribute to contentment, and of measuring this contentment according to the perfections that give rise to pleasures, and of dispassionately judging these perfections and these pleasures, will ensure them from many faults. But, in order to thus estimate the goods, we must know them perfectly; and

---

15. AT IV, 288–90.
16. Descartes to Elisabeth (August 4, 1645), AT IV, 266.

to know all those from which we are constrained to make a choice in an active life, we would need necessarily to possess infinite knowledge. You will say that we will not fail to be satisfied if our conscience testifies that we took all possible precautions. But this never happens when we cannot find out more. For we always change our mind about things that remain to be considered. To measure the contentment according to the perfection that causes it, we would need to see clearly the value of each thing, whether those serving us alone, or those rendering us still more useful to others, are preferable. The latter seem to be esteemed with an excess of humor by people who torment themselves about others, and the former by people who only live for themselves. And, nevertheless, each of them supports his inclination with reasons strong enough to make it persist all through his life. It is likewise with the other perfections of body and mind: a tacit sentiment makes reason endorse. This sentiment should not be called a passion since it is with us from birth. Therefore, please tell me, how it should be followed (since it is a gift of nature), and how to correct it.

I would still like to see you define the passions, in order to understand them well; for those who call them perturbations of the soul would persuade me that the force of the passions consists only in obscuring and subjecting reason, if experience did not show me that some of them lead us to reasonable actions. But I am sure you will shed more light on this for me when you explain how the strength of the passions makes them that much more useful when they are subject to reason.

Elisabeth to Descartes (September 30 [1645])[17]

Knowledge of the existence of God and his attributes[18] can console us from the misfortunes that come to us from the ordinary course of nature and in the order he established there, such as losing well-being because of storms, health by an infection of the air, friends through death; but it cannot console us from those misfortunes imposed on us by humans, whose will appears to us entirely free, there being faith alone to persuade us that God takes care to govern volitions, and that he determined the fortune of each person before the creation of the world.

---

17. AT IV, 302–3.
18. Descartes to Elisabeth (September 15, 1645), AT IV, 291.

The immortality of the soul, and the knowledge that it is many times more noble than the body,[19] is capable of having us seek death just as well as despising it, since we could not doubt that we will live more happily exempt from the illnesses and passions of the body. And I am surprised that those who said they were convinced of this truth and lived without revealed law, preferred an arduous life to an advantageous death.

The great extent of the universe,[20] which you showed in book III of your *Principles*, serves to detach our affections from what we see of it; but it also separates this particular providence, which is the foundation of theology, from the idea we have of God.

The consideration that we are a part of the whole, whose advantage we must seek,[21] is surely the source of all generous actions; but I find many difficulties in the conditions you prescribe for them. How do we measure the harms we bring upon ourselves on behalf of the public against the good that will come from it, without these harms seeming greater to us to the extent our idea of them is more distinct? And what rule will we have for comparing things that are not equally well known to us, such as our own merit and the merit of those with whom we live? Someone naturally arrogant will always tip the balance to his side, and someone modest will esteem himself less than he is worth.

In order to profit from the specific truths of which you speak,[22] we must understand exactly all these passions and all these preoccupations, most of which are not perceptible. In observing the customs of the country in which we live, we sometimes find some very unreasonable ones, which it is necessary to follow in order to avoid greater difficulties.

Elisabeth to Descartes (October 28 [1645])[23]

After having given such good reasons to show that it is better to know truths disadvantageous to us than to pleasantly fool ourselves, and that only the things susceptible to different, equally true, considerations oblige us to settle upon the ones that will bring us more contentment. Thus, I am surprised you wish me to compare myself to those of my age in something

---

19. Ibid, AT IV, 292.
20. Ibid.
21. Ibid., AT IV, 293.
22. Ibid., AT IV, 294.
23. AT IV, 321–24.

unknown to me rather than something I cannot fail to know, even though the latter would be more to my advantage.[24] There is nothing that can enlighten me as to whether I profited more, in cultivating my reason, than others did in pursuing their ambitions, and I do not doubt that, with the time for relaxation that my body would require, more time would remain for me to advance beyond what I am now. If we measured the scope of the human mind through the example of common people, it would be found to have very little extension, because most people use thought only with regard to the senses. Even for those who apply themselves to study, there are few who use it for anything but memory or who have truth as the goal of their labor. So, if there is a vice in my not taking pleasure in considering whether I gained more than these people, I do not think it is an excess of humility, which is just as harmful as presumption, but not as ordinary. We are more inclined to misjudge our defects than our perfections. And, in fleeing from regret for errors we committed, as if it were an enemy of felicity, we could run the risk of losing the desire to correct ourselves, especially when some passion produced them, since we naturally like to be moved by them and to follow their motions; it is only the difficulties that follow, as a result, that teach us such errors can be harmful. And this is, in my judgment, the reason tragedies please more, to the extent they excite more sadness, because we know that this sadness will not be violent enough to lead us to extravagances, nor last long enough to corrupt our health.

But this does not suffice to support the doctrine contained in one of your previous letters, that the passions are even more useful as they tend more toward excess, when they are subject to reason, because it seems they cannot be both excessive and subject to reason.[25] But I think you will clarify this doubt by taking the trouble to describe how this particular agitation of the spirits serves to form all the passions we experience, and in what way it corrupts our reasoning. I would not dare ask this of you if I did not know you never leave any work imperfect, and that in undertaking to teach a stupid person like me, you prepared yourself for the difficulties this would bring you.

It is what makes me continue and tell you that the reasons proving the existence of God and that he is the immutable cause of all the effects which do not depend upon human free will do not persuade me that he is also

---

24. See Descartes to Elisabeth (October 6, 1645), AT IV, 306.
25. See Descartes to Elisabeth (September 13, 1645), AT IV, 287.

the cause of those that do depend on it.²⁶ It follows necessarily from his supreme perfection that he could be this cause, that is, that he could not have given free will to humans; but, since we feel that we have free will, it seems to me that it is repugnant to common sense to think it dependent in its operations, as it is in its being.

If we are quite persuaded of the immortality of the soul, it is impossible to doubt that the soul will be happier after its separation from the body (which is the origin of all the displeasure of life, as the soul is of the greatest contentment), except for Mr. Digby's opinion,²⁷ whose teacher²⁸ (whose writings you saw) made him believe in the necessity of Purgatory, by persuading him that the passions dominating reason during man's life leave some vestiges in the soul, after the death of the body. These vestiges torment the soul all the more in that they find no means of satisfying themselves in so pure a substance. I do not see how that accords with the immateriality of the soul. But I do not doubt that, although life is not bad of itself, it must be abandoned for a condition that we will know to be better.

By this special providence, which is the foundation of theology,²⁹ I understand the one by which God from all eternity prescribed means so strange as his incarnation, for a part of the whole creation, which is so insignificant compared to the value of the rest (in the same way as you represent this globe for us in your physics). He did all this in order to be glorified for it, which seems an end quite unworthy for the creator of this great universe. But here I presented to you the objection of our theologians rather than my own, having always believed it is most irrelevant for finite people to judge the final cause of the actions of an infinite being.

You do not think we need an exact knowledge of the extent to which reason demands we interest ourselves on behalf of the public, because insofar as each person relates everything to himself, he will also be working for others if he made use of prudence. And this prudence is the whole, of which I ask you only for a part. For, by possessing it, we could not fail to do justice to others as to ourselves; an absence of prudence is the reason why a freethinker might sometimes lose the means to serve his country by

---

26. See Descartes to Elisabeth (October 6, 1645), AT IV, 313–14.
27. See Elisabeth to Descartes (May 24 [1645]), AT IV, 209.
28. Thomas White? See ibid., AT IV, 210.
29. See Descartes to Elisabeth (October 6, 1645), AT IV, 315.

abandoning himself too freely to his interest, and a timid person might lose himself along with his country for failing to risk his goods and fortune for its preservation.

Elisabeth to Descartes [November 30, 1645][30]

You will have cause to be surprised that, after having told me that my reasoning did not appear entirely ridiculous to you, I remain such a long time without reaping the benefit your replies offer me. And it is with shame that I confess the cause to you, since it overturned everything that your lessons seemed to have established in my mind. I thought that a firm resolution to seek happiness only in the things that depend on my will would make me less sensitive to those coming to me from elsewhere, before the folly of one of my brothers made me recognize my weakness. For it upset the health of my body and the tranquility of my soul more than all the misfortunes that have yet beset me. [. . .]

IV, 335

I likewise confess to you, that although I do not understand how the independence of free will is any less repugnant to our idea of God than its dependence is to its freedom,[31] it is impossible for me to reconcile them, it being as impossible for the will to be at the same time free and attached to the decrees of providence, as for divine power to be both infinite and limited. I do not see their compatibility of which you speak, nor how this dependence of the will can be of another nature than its freedom if you do not take the trouble of teaching it to me.

336

With respect to contentment,[32] I confess that its present possession is much more certain than its future expectation, regardless of the good reason on which that expectation is founded. But I have trouble convincing myself that we always have more goods than ills in life, since it takes more to make up the former than the latter: people have more occasion to receive displeasure than pleasure; there are an infinite number of errors for just a single truth; there are so many ways to go astray, and just one path that leads in the right direction; so many people with the intent and the power to harm and few who possess both to serve. In the end, everything depending on will and the course of the rest of the world can disturb us;

337

---

30. AT IV, 335–37.
31. See Descartes to Elisabeth (November 3, 1645), AT IV, 332.
32. Ibid., AT IV, 333.

and, according to your own opinion, only what depends absolutely on our own will is sufficient to give us real and constant satisfaction.

Elisabeth to Descartes (April 25 [1646])[33]

I was prevented until now from making good on the permission you gave me to detail for you the obscurities that my own stupidity leads me to find in your *Treatise on the Passions*. However, they are few in number, since one would have to be insensible not to understand that the order, definition, and distinctions you give to the passions, and indeed the entire moral part of the treatise, surpass anything anyone ever said on the subject.

But since the physical part is not so clear to the ignorant, I do not see how one can know the different motions of the blood that cause the five primitive passions, since those passions never occur in isolation. For example, love is always accompanied with desire and joy, or desire and sadness, and as it strengthens the others grow as well, . . .[34] on the contrary. How, therefore, is it possible to notice the difference in the beating of the pulse, the digestion of foods, and other bodily changes that serve to discover the nature of these motions? Moreover, what you observe in each of these passions is not the same in all temperaments: mine is such that sadness always takes away my appetite, although it is never mixed with hatred, being occasioned only by the death of a friend.

When you speak of the external signs of these passions, you say that admiration combined with joy makes the lungs expand in irregular fits, causing laughter. To this I beg you to add the way in which admiration (which, according to your description, seems to only operate on the brain) can so readily open the orifices of the heart to achieve this effect.

These passions, which you cite as the cause of sighs, do not seem to always be so, since custom and the stomach being filled also produce them.

But I find still less difficulty understanding everything you say about the passions than practicing the remedies you give against their excesses. For how can one predict all the accidents that can arise in life, which are impossible to enumerate? And how can we prevent ourselves from ardently desiring the things that necessarily tend toward the conservation of people (such as health and the means for living), which nevertheless do not depend on one's free will? As for knowledge of the truth, the desire

---

33. AT IV, 404–5.
34. Gap in the text.

for it is so just that it is naturally in all people; but we would need infinite knowledge to know the just value of the goods and ills that have the habit of moving us, since there are many more than a single person could imagine, and we would need for this to have perfect knowledge of everything in the world.

From the Letters between Descartes and Chanut

Descartes to Chanut (June 15, 1646)[35]

Since it pleases you to take the trouble of rereading my *Principles* and examining them, I am sure you will notice many obscurities and many errors that are very important for me to know, and about which I cannot hope to be made aware as well by anyone but you. I only fear that you would get tired of this reading because what I wrote only distantly relates to morality, which you have chosen as your principal area of study.

It is not that I am not entirely of your opinion, insofar as you judge that the most certain method of knowing how we should live is first to know who we are, what is the world in which we live, and who is the creator of this world, or who is the master of the house in which we live. But, aside from the fact that I neither claim nor promise, in any way, that everything I wrote is true, there is a very wide gap between the general notions of the heavens and earth, which I tried to give in my *Principles*, and knowledge of the nature of man in particular, which I still did not treat. However, in order that it not seem that I want to discourage you from your plan, I will tell you, in confidence, that the notion of physics I tried to develop served me tremendously in establishing foundations in morals that are certain; I more easily satisfied myself on this point than on many others concerning medicine, on which I nevertheless spent much more time. As such, instead of finding the means for preserving life, I found something else, easier, and surer, which is to not fear death;[36] and to do so, however, without being chagrined, as are typically those whose wisdom is completely derived from the teachings of others, and which rests on foundations that depend only on prudence and the authority of men.

IV, 441

442

---

35. AT IV, 441–42.
36. See also Descartes to Huygens (June 6, 1639), AT II, 682.

I will tell you further that, while I let the plants in my garden grow, for which I am waiting for some experiments to try to continue my Physics, I also pause from time to time to think on specific questions in morals. Thus, I sketched a little *Treatise on the Nature of the Passions of the Soul* this winter,[37] without, however, having any plans to publish it, and I would be of a mind to write still something else if my distaste in seeing just how few people in the world deign to read my writings did not cause me to be negligent.

Chanut to Descartes (August 25, 1646)[38]

I do not claim that the path you found for the establishment of some moral principles, through knowledge of physics, can never serve me: I do not feel strong enough to walk in your footsteps; but I am delighted, on the one hand, to learn that it is thus not impossible to have something firm and certain on this subject, about which I often doubted, having found nothing in books that satisfied me; and, on the other hand, I nearly dare to hope that charity will persuade you some day to communicate it to the public, without considering whether those predisposed to the opinions of the School or to jealousy deserve it, but thinking of the inestimable good to be derived by those who, in the future, will study true wisdom. If God arranged my life such that I might spend a part of it near you, I would hope that you would not refuse something of this to me, even before the public might have received it; but, in the state I am in, I do not ask for it, and even judge that such things are not easily explained in parcels and through letters. I cannot hide from you that, of all things human, I value nothing as much as this knowledge and that, if I thought an entire year's meditation might give me a single well-assured foundation, I would leave behind all other work for this acquisition: not to make a parade of it, but for my personal use and the direction of my life.

I experienced another joy in your letter, where I noticed a change with respect to the distaste you displayed when in Amsterdam; given that you wrote something on the passions of the soul, you are no longer angry with us, and are committed to doing us even more good. For I believe, Sir, that I reason well, judging rightly that it is not possible for these most common actions of the soul to be known exactly, that we penetrated the very nature

---

37. See Elisabeth to Descartes (April 25 [1646]), AT IV, 404–6.
38. AT IV, 601–3.

of the soul and its connection with the body, things that until now are well hidden mysteries. And it is in this connection that I interpret what you add, that you will gladly write something further.

Chanut to Descartes (December 1, 1646)[39]

On the subject of love, I need, Sir, to confess frankly my ignorance: after reading a thousand beautiful things on it in the Ancients, I remained as before with some light, feeling the matter very pleasant and necessary, but not knowing it at all. I experience, like other people, the joys and the sweetness of this passion; but, to speak the truth, I do not know it well and could not precisely determine what this motion of the soul is. So many different sorts of appetite, so many inclinations with no apparent reason, such a great number of objects of enjoyments so bizarre all confuse me, such that I resolve to love whatever I think merits it, without informing myself any further.

But there is a difficulty that sometimes bothers me and which I will reveal to you all the more willingly, since, to ease my pain, charity will incite you to tell me in this encounter, that which you would not do for a simple curiosity. I clearly feel, when I listen to reason, that we must love God; I speak about this in terms of a purely moral investigation, without the assistance of Christian truth and the grace of God that comes with it. But all the measures and the reasons for affection seem to me so lacking that I hardly understand how this action of our soul toward an object infinite in every way might be called anything else but astonishment and very respectful confusion. I do not know if I am mistaken, and I beg you to disabuse me of this thought if my remark is false; but it seems to me that none of the philosophers dared to say that people must love God, and that this familiarity of the creature toward God is a principle of religion.

Moreover, Sir, although before reading your *Principles* I did not know what light was, I was still able to see at least as clearly as I do at present; and thus, although I admit I do not in any way know the nature of love, I am not insensitive to it, especially where you are concerned. And it is what gives me most difficulty, feeling in myself such a great effort and not knowing what moves me so violently. I know quite well what causes this affection in me, I feel its effects, I guard it as the sweetest sentiment in my soul; and with all that, I do not in truth know what it is. [. . .]

---

39. AT IV, 610–13.

The last time I had the honor of seeing the Queen, one of her affairs gave her occasion to fall upon a question about which she required me to give my opinion; I will gladly include it here, because it is not distant from what I was saying to you at the beginning of this letter, and it will show you that her mind is quite elevated, namely: "Which of two disorders and ill uses is worse, that of love or that of hatred?" The question was general, and the term "love" was understood in the fashion of the philosophers, and not in the way it is made so often to ring in the ears of girls. I dared, on this question, to take a side contrary to her thinking, and my protest got her to say several things of great wisdom and subtle reasoning.

Chanut to Descartes (May 11, 1647)[40]

You would have had a prompt reply to the letter you graciously wrote to me February 1, if it had been as easy for me to understand it as the little it cost you to put it down on paper. It is not that I found any resistance in my mind to giving my consent: my belief in you alone disposes me to receive anything from you without discussion. But, in order that I might profit more from what you give me, I want to study it with discernment, and for that I need time—in truth, not very much time, but I need to be calm and free from the agitation of other thoughts, and I am not often in a position to enjoy such favorable circumstances. The first time I found myself with the freedom to give myself to this agreeable reading without interruption, I was so delighted by it that a few days later I could not refocus my mind on the business at hand; and as my soul was full of these notions I received with so much pleasure, it happened that the Queen of Sweden's physician, a wise and very honest man named Mr. du Rier, came to pay me a visit. Right away I unburdened my heart to him and told him of my joy. I reread to him, without his becoming bored, this eight-page letter, which he admired no less than I did, and he asked me to loan it to him for some time to consider it at leisure. I politely refused this request, not wanting to give up such a precious text. But a few days later, I was pressed by the Queen, to whom he talked about it, to show it to her. I was very pleased that her Majesty had this curiosity, so that by reading this single piece, she would know that everything I told her about you was still an underestimation of your true worth. It is also true, Sir, that, flattery aside, her judgment is so clear and so detached from all concerns, that I do not think there is anything in

---

40. AT X, 618–24.

philosophy she could not understand with ease. I delayed from one audience to the next until I could find free time not taken up by other matters; and although she asked for your letter for several days, I excused myself to have it read to her at a convenient time. After listening to it, she remained so satisfied that she could not stop singing your praises and inquiring after all the details of your life and person. I told her everything I knew; and after thinking a little about it, she concluded: "Mr. Descartes, as I see him in this letter, and as you depict him for me, is the most fortunate of all men, and his condition seems worthy of envy; you will do me the pleasure of assuring him of the great esteem in which I hold him." I am not reporting to you here everything her Majesty said on all the points of your letter, which she did not have me read uninterruptedly; on the contrary, she often stopped me to confirm through her reasoning what she was understanding very well; and I assure you, Sir, that I was no less surprised by the ease with which she penetrated into your thinking than I was by their profundity at my first reading of them.

On the first question, where you explain in general the nature of love, her Majesty paid close attention but did not wish to invest in examining the doctrine "because," she said, "not having experienced this passion, she could not judge a painting well whose original she did not know." I remained in agreement that she did not know love as a passion; but I think that, if she wanted, she could have spoken quite aptly of intellectual love, which is concerned with a pure good separate from perceivable things, because, generally, I do not believe anyone in the world is more affected by the love of virtue.

Finally, after hearing everything, she did not refuse to consent to any of your opinions, except for one line in which you suppose the world to be infinitely extended. [. . .]

However, Sir, I must warn you that I am of a humor to want to find my part in all the affairs that pass through my hands; and, persuading myself that I will do you a service when I will show the Queen your reply to her concern, I ask that you please recognize my intervention with some liberality; and in order that you not trouble yourself to find a gift that is suitable, I will freely tell you what I would wish for.

I do not see clearly what is this secret impulse that leads us to befriend one person rather than another before even knowing their merit; and although it seems to me I do not know what confused opinion of the goodness of the object attracting us can be its cause, my difficulty remains insofar as, while I do not know clearly what marks and what signs put forward this opinion, I wonder whether this hidden allegiance has its origin in the body or in the mind. If it arises from the body, I would like to understand it better than through the general terms of sympathy and antipathy, with which our Scholastic philosophers hide their ignorance; and, if the attraction of friendship comes from the disposition of our souls in their own substance, although it appears outside of human ability to give any reason for it, I am so accustomed to learning from you what I thought was impossible to know that I do not despair your giving me some satisfaction. But, according to my ordinary method, I intend to bring the knowledge you will give me down to the conduct of my life in order to live better; and, for that I ask you, Sir, whether a good man can, in the choice of his friendships, follow these hidden motions of his heart and his mind, which have no apparent reason, and whether he does not commit an injustice in distributing his inclinations through some other rule than that of merit. This question exercised my mind more than once, insofar as, in separating friendship from two things we often confuse with it, one being the esteem of virtue, and the other being this mutual exchange of favors with honest people, which is indeed only a trading of benefits, friendship remains as a simple link and a cement assembling all people in a single body and which must be of equal force among all the parts; otherwise, it is impossible for there ever to arise divisions against natural equity, and that, by attaching ourselves too strongly to some people, we are imperceptibly separated from others. I do not think we can refuse the title of sage to anyone making as a foundation in his heart an equal love for all humans, since they are all equally human; this would only add to it distinctions of merit and the obligation of recognition in the traffic of favors. And, although the esteem of virtue and rewarding of good deeds might make it appear that a person loves someone more than another, because these three affections blend together very easily and appear to only produce a single motion, it would however be true that he would have for all but one very equal friendship.

Descartes to Chanut (November 20, 1647)[41]

It is true that I usually refuse to write down my thoughts concerning morality. There are two reasons for this. One is that there is no other matter

---

41. AT V, 86–88.

on which malicious people can more easily derive pretexts for slandering; the other is that I believe it belongs only to sovereigns, or those authorized by them, to concern themselves in regulating the customs of others. But these two reasons do not apply to the opportunity you did me the honor of giving me, by writing on behalf of the incomparable Queen whom you serve, that it pleases her if I write to her about my opinion regarding the supreme good. This command authorizes me sufficiently, but I hope that what I write will only be seen by her and you. I wish with such passion to obey her that, far from being reserved, I would like to be able to include in a letter everything I ever thought on this subject. In fact, I wanted to put so many things in the one I hazarded writing to her[42] that I fear I did not explain anything sufficiently in it. But, to make up for this defect, I am sending you a collection of some other letters[43] in which I give a fuller treatment of the same things. And I include a little *Treatise on the Passions*, which is not the least part of the collection; for it is primarily the passions we must try to understand in order to obtain the supreme good I described. If I also dared to include the replies that I had the honor of receiving from the Princess to whom these letters are addressed,[44] this collection would have been more complete, and I could yet have added two or three of mine, which are not intelligible without hers; but I would have had to ask her for permission, and she is now quite far from here.

The Tree of Philosophy[45]

I noticed on examining the nature of many different minds that there are almost none of them so dull or slow of understanding that they are incapable of sound opinions, and even of attaining all the highest sciences if they were trained in the right way. And this may also be proved by reason. For, since the principles are clear and nothing must be deduced from them

---

42. Descartes to Christina (November 20, 1647), AT V, 81–86.
43. Descartes to Elisabeth (July 21, 1645), AT IV, 251–53, (August 4, 1645), AT IV, 263–68, (August 18, 1645), AT IV, 271–78, (September 1, 1645), AT IV, 281–87, (September 15, 1645), AT IV, 290–96, and (October 6, 1645), AT IV, 304–17.
44. That is, Elisabeth to Descartes (August 16 [1645]), AT IV, 268–70, [August 1645], AT IV, 278–80, (September 13 [1645]), AT IV, 288–90, (September 30 [1645]), AT IV, 301–4, and (October 28 [1645]), AT IV, 321–24.
45. From the Preface to *Principles of Philosophy* (French edition, 1647), AT IXb, 12–16.

except by very evident reasoning, we all have sufficient intelligence to understand the conclusions that depend on them. But in addition to the drawbacks of prejudice from which no one is entirely exempt (although it is those who have studied bad science the most who are most harmed), it almost always happens that those of moderate intelligence neglect to study because they do not consider themselves capable of doing so, and that the others who are more eager hasten on too quickly. And from this it comes that they often accept principles that are not really evident, and from them derive consequences that are uncertain. That is why I want to assure those who too greatly disparage their powers that there is nothing in my writings they are not capable of understanding completely if they take the trouble to examine them; while I also warn the others that even the most superior minds will require much time and attention to understand all the matters which I intended to include in them.

Following on this, and to make very clear the end I had in view in publishing them, I would like to explain here what seems to me to be the order that should be followed in our self-instruction. To begin with, a person who as yet has merely common and imperfect knowledge [...] should above all try to form for himself a code of morals sufficient to regulate the actions of his life, because this does not permit any delay, and we ought above all other things to endeavor to live well. After that he should likewise study logic—not the logic of the Schools, because properly speaking it is only a dialectic that teaches how to make the things we know understood by others, or even to repeat, without forming any judgment on them, many words respecting those we do not know, thus corrupting rather than increasing good sense—but the logic that teaches us how best to direct our reason in order to discover those truths of which we are ignorant. And since this is very dependent on custom, it is good for him to practice the rules for a long time on easy and simple questions such as those of mathematics. Then, when he has acquired a certain skill in discovering the truth in these questions, he should begin seriously to apply himself to the true philosophy, the first part of which is metaphysics, containing the principles of knowledge, among which is the explanation of the principal attributes of God, the immateriality of our souls, and all the clear and simple notions that are in us. The second is physics, in which, after having found the true principles of material things, we examine generally how the whole universe is composed, and then in particular what is the nature of this earth and of all the bodies most commonly found around it, such as air, water, and fire, magnetic ore, and other minerals. It is then necessary to inquire individually into the nature of plants, animals, and above all man, so that we may afterward be able to discover the other sciences useful to man. Thus, philosophy as a whole is like a tree whose roots are metaphysics, whose trunk is physics, and whose branches, which issue from this trunk, are all the other sciences. These reduce themselves to three principal ones, namely, medicine, mechanics, and morals—by morals I mean the highest and most perfect moral science which, presupposing a complete knowledge of the other sciences, is the ultimate degree of wisdom.

But just as it is not from the roots or the trunk of trees that one gathers the fruit, but only from the extremities of their branches, so the main use of philosophy is dependent on those of its parts that we cannot learn until the end. Although, however, I am ignorant of almost all of these, the zeal I always showed in trying to render service to the public caused me to print ten or twelve years ago certain essays on things I appeared to have learned. The first part of these essays was a *Discourse on the Method of Rightly Conducting One's Reason and Seeking Truth in the Sciences*, in which I summarized the principal rules of logic and of an imperfect system of morals which may be followed provisionally while we still know none better. The other parts were three treatises: the first *Dioptrics*; the second *Meteors*, and the last *Geometry*. In the *Dioptrics* I intended to show that we could make sufficient progress in philosophy to attain by its means a knowledge of those arts useful to life, because the invention of the telescope, which I there explained, is one of the most difficult ever attempted. In the treatise on *Meteors*, I endeavored to make clear the difference between the philosophy I cultivate and the one taught in the Schools, where the same subject is usually treated. Finally in the *Geometry* I professed to show that I found certain matters of which people were previously ignorant, and thus to afford occasion for believing that many more may yet be discovered, in order by this means to incite all people to the search after truth. From this time onward, foreseeing the difficulty which would be felt by many in understanding the foundations of metaphysics, I tried to explain the principal points in a book of *Meditations* which is not very large, but whose volume was increased, and whose matter was much illuminated, by the objections many very learned persons sent me regarding them, and by the replies I made to them. Then, finally, when it appeared to me that these preceding treatises sufficiently prepared the mind of readers to accept the *Principles of Philosophy*, I likewise published them, and I divided the book containing them into four parts, the first of which contains the principles of knowledge, which is what may be called First Philosophy or Metaphysics. That is why it is better to read beforehand the Meditations which I wrote on the same subject, in order that it may be properly understood. The other three parts contain what is most general in Physics, that is, an explanation of the first laws or principles of nature, the manner in which the heavens, fixed stars, planets, comets, and generally the whole of universe are composed. Then the nature of this earth, and of air, water, fire, and magnetic ore is dealt with more particularly, for these are the bodies that may most commonly be found everywhere around it, as also all the qualities observed in these bodies, such as light, heat, weight, and the like. By this means I believe myself to have begun to explain all of philosophy in sequence, without having omitted anything that ought to precede the last things of which I wrote. But to carry this plan to a conclusion, I should afterward in the same way explain in further detail the nature of each of the other bodies on the earth, that is, minerals, plants, animals, and above all man, then finally treat exactly of medicine, morals, and mechanics. All this I should have to do in order to give to mankind a complete body of philosophy; I do not feel myself to be so old, I do not so much despair of my strength, and I do not find myself so far removed from a knowledge of what remains that I should not venture to endeavor to achieve this design, if I had the means of making all the experiments I would need in order to support and justify my reasoning. But seeing that great expense is requisite for this end, to which the resources of an individual like myself could not attain if he were not given assistance by the public, and not seeing that I can expect that aid, I conceive it to be henceforth my duty to content myself with studying for my own private instruction, trusting that posterity will excuse me if I fail henceforth to work on its behalf.

From a Prefatory Letter to the *Passions of the Soul*[46]

I admit that I took longer in revising the little treatise I am sending you[47] than I did in composing it, and that, however, I added very little to it, and

---

46. AT XI, 326.
47. The letter addresses an anonymous correspondent (referred to as "one of Descartes's friends"), whose two letters, along with Descartes's replies, are used as a preface to the volume (AT XI, 301–26).

changed nothing in the discourse, whose simplicity and brevity will reveal that my purpose was not to explain the passions as an orator, or even as a moral philosopher, but only as a physicist. So, I foresee that this treatise will fare no better than my other writings; and although its title may invite more people to read it, it will nevertheless satisfy only those who take the trouble to examine it carefully. Such as it is, I place it in your hands.

Egmont, August 14, 1649

Concerning the *Treatise on the Passions*[48]

I will not extend myself further in thanking you for all the care and precautions you graciously took, so that the letters[49] I had the honor of receiving from the land of the North did not fail to fall into my hands. I am so well obliged to you and have so many other proofs of your friendship, that it is not new to me. I will only say that no letter was lost, and that I am resolved to make the trip to which the last letters invited me, even though I was more reluctant at first than you could perhaps have imagined. The trip I made to Paris last summer put me off; and I can assure you that the extraordinary esteem I have for Mr. Chanut and the assurance I have of his friendship are not the least important reasons that caused my resolve.

    As for the *Treatise on the Passions*, I have no hope that it will be published before I am in Sweden; for I was negligent in revising it, and adding the things you thought lacking, which will increase it by a third; for it will contain three parts, the first of which will deal with passions in general, and at times with the nature of the soul, etc., the second with the six primitive passions, and the third with all the others.

---

48. From Descartes to Clerselier [April 23, 1649], AT V, 353–54.
49. Christina to Descartes (December 12, 1648), AT V, 251–52, Chanut to Descartes (December 12, 1648), AT V, 252–54, and Chanut to Descartes (February 27, 1649), AT V, 296–97.